THE ROMAN EMPIRE

A Concise History of the First Two Centuries

Robert N. Schwartz

University Press of America,® Inc.
Lanham • New York • Oxford

Copyright © 1998
University Press of America,® Inc.
4720 Boston Way
Lanham, Maryland 20706

12 Hid's Copse Rd.
Cummor Hill, Oxford OX2 9JJ

Library of Congress Cataloging-in-Publication Data

Schwartz, Robert N.
The Roman Empire : a concise history of the first two centuries /
Robert N. Schwartz.
p.   cm.
Includes bibliographical references and index.
l. Rome—History—Empire, 30 B. C.-284 A. D.   I. Title.
DG276.S34 1998   936'.06—dc21   98-7817 CIP

ISBN 0-7618-1172-9 (cloth: alk. ppr.)
ISBN 0-7618-1173-7 (pbk: alk. ppr.)

ACKNOWLEDGMENTS

I gratefully acknowledge the assistance of both people and institutions in the course of completing this manuscript. A Rockefeller Foreign Language Fellowship allowed me to study at the American Academy in Rome in 1990. There the ruins of the Roman Empire fired my imagination and fueled a determination to share my explorations through a concise history of the Empire. An Arthur Patch McKinley grant from the American Classical League in 1993 allowed me to take a megastep toward completing the chapters. The libraries of the University of Florida, the University of Houston and the Central Florida Community Colege furnished me with ample research materials and a peaceful environment. Special thanks to Cambridge University Press for permission to reproduce their excellent maps.

I wish to recognize the assistance of former students, now graduates of the University of Texas and Texas A&M University, together with teachers, professors, colleagues and laymen. Each of them contributed immensely to making this book possible and encouraged me to see it to completion: Howard and Carol Parsonage, Maria Carla Geiger, Claudia Madeira, Paul Yozzo, Ben Moon, Ibrahim Alsaeed, Matt Matejich, Curtis Neason, Darlend, Helen L. Eaker, Debra Powers, Chris Kanolis, Lorene Pouncey, Rachel Reed, Ron Tetrick, David L. Thompson, my brother, Jim Schwartz, and in a special way, my wife, Irene. *Gratias vobis ago*!

The temple to the deified Antoninus and Faustina, AD 141,
embodies the power and glory of Rome.

Dedicated to the men, women and children
who were wantonly sacrificed
on the altar of civilization
from time immemorial
to our era.
May some at least now learn
from the past.

CONTENTS

Part One
The First Century: A Time of Youth

Part Two
The Second Century: A Time of Maturing

The Five Good Emperors (AD 96-180)

EPILOGUE

Maps

1. The Roman Empire under Hadrian
2. Central Europe
3. Roman Germany
4. The Danube Lands
5. Spain
6. North Africa

Illustrations
Taken from "A Walking Tour of Rome"
by the author.

The Julio-Claudian Family
(following Chapter II)

PREFACE

This book is a user-friendly introduction to the world of the Romans. It focuses on the people of the Roman Empire and their lives, all of them united by a common bond, the Latin language. Whether emperors, senators, knights, generals or bureaucrats, tribesmen or nations, slaves, cultists or the common man, whose presence was everywhere: all molded the Roman Empire into a lasting memorial, known to us through Latin and the arts of learning. Because the study of Latin is so closely bound to the Empire, with its people and their challenges, the Latin student cannot afford to ignore the culture and history of that era. The language follows the people, much as their shadow, which cannot exist alone.

It is my intent to recount the exciting story of how the Empire was formed, who the role players were, and what lessons their lives may have for student and layman today. My efforts were inspired by my Latin students. Their competitive juices were whetted in many a contest, which they know as a *certamen.* The certamen requires a knowledge of the men and events of Roman history. Yet, at each event, whether at regional or state level, the students had to memorize detached and unrelated facts, floating in a kind of limbo. This left them little room to understand and enjoy what was really happening in the Empire. This book was written to solve that problem by bringing together the rich record of the past, so that the reader will find more meaning in his study of Latin, as well as an interest in his whole Western heritage.

The Latin language was the tool of living people who shaped the past. They carried that tool the length and width of the Mediterranean world, touching upon three continents and engulfing millions of peoples in a harmonious effort that produced the *pax Romana*, the Roman peace. Latin became the lingua franca two thousand years ago, not because the language was forced on the non-native speakers, but because so many saw it as a strategic second language. It was a cherished tool for all who learned it, whether student, businessman, tribal official or those who found themselves living close by a legionary camp.

A command of Latin enabled students to learn about the history, law and poetry of the leading nation of their time. Businessmen, armed with Latin, could better understand market needs in distant cities and be the first to strike profitable deals abroad. Tribal leaders could clearly express their needs and interests, gaining the confidence of Roman officials. This landed them in good positions within the bureaucracy and military and got them appointments to high places. In short, the Latin language gave power. It also led the individual beyond his immediate surroundings, into a broader world of ideas and things.

Today, our lives make even greater use of the entire Roman heritage. Our inheritance from the Roman Empire necessarily includes art and architecture, engineering and a long list of other accomplishments. The use of concrete, the development of law courts, schooling--even government itself--these are part and parcel of our daily lives. All were part of theirs, as well.

A history of the Roman people must not fail to paint a personal portrait of the men and women who were role-players of that era, either. Such a history will, in summary, reflect the rays of learning that began layering in 753 B.C. and continued until A.D. 476. Like bookends, the two dates define an era that laid a foundation so deep that we call it "Classical."

The storied past of Rome is one we still play out in our daily lives, whether consciously or not. Our Senate and bicameral legislatures, our consular service, civil codes, coinage and taxation, public welfare and care for orphans owe much to Roman civilization. And our cities, with their grid patterns, plazas, columns and arches, our palaces, atriums and churches, roads, bridges and stadiums, even our drain pipes and commodes reflect Roman engineering and its inventive use of concrete.

The many sayings that appear in all languages today, such as: "Actions speak louder than words!" "Time flies!" and "Seize the moment!" are simply timeworn hand-me-downs from the Romans' *"facta non verba," "tempus fugit"* and *"carpe diem,"* respectively.

Today there are regional trends towards union among nations, whether for cultural, economic or security reasons. But emperor Caracalla set the early standard when in A.D. 212 he made all free persons, from Britain to Mesopotamia, citizens of the Empire. What a feeling it must have been at that time for Nile River oarsmen to be able to visit fishermen along the Seine River in Paris and chat about the latest trends in jewelry coming from Cologne glassmakers along the Rhine. No passports necessary! The traveler needed but an adventurous spirit and a strong pair of legs. A network of roads was in place that he could follow in all directions.

One of the most amazing features of the Empire lay in its road system. Developed by advancing armies, roads networked to every sizable city and town. They circled the Mediterranean, penetrated the world's driest deserts, the Negev and Arabian to the east, and skirted the Sahara to the west. The merchant who so chose could sail westward from Alexandria, Egypt, to Cyrene, Libya. From there he could follow a road, by donkey or horseback, clear across northern Africa until he curved around the Atlas mountains before finally reaching the shores of the Atlantic at Rabat, Morocco. That was in an earlier time. Today's obstacles to similar travel make deserts and mountain ranges seem like mere stepping-stones.

This was the world seen through Roman eyes. But the peoples that made up the Empire were not of interchangeable races, faces, clothing styles and tastes. Just the opposite. Their appearances, languages, religions and foods spoke of different ways of life, one from another, even under the Romans. Still, they held fast to the notion that Roman government was there to protect them. Their citizenship assured them the support of the law and the security of power. Their taxes confirmed their privileges: a hearing in the law courts, and guarantees of the right to work, worship and live as they chose, though clearly there were exceptions. They could even appeal for justice directly to the emperor, if the need arose. It was an advantage for them to know one of the two major languages, Latin or Greek, besides their own.

The exchange of commodities like fruits, vegetables, meats and spices, dishware, silverware, jewelry and clothing crossed the borders of all forty-four provinces without taxes. So did the intellectual commodities of literature, drama, math, sciences and religious sects. Art and technology, too, like musical instruments, boat-building, waterproof concrete, sculpture, fresco painting, mosaics, plant and animal use: each contributed to an endless list, each helping tie the threads of mankind into a multicolored fabric suitable for its time.

Today it awakens a spirit of yearning when we think of how unity was achieved in diversity. Warfare between provinces was unheard of. Differences were a source of fascination. It wasn't until the shadow of the Roman *fasces* faded into the twilight of chaos that kings, czars, princes and sheiks rose to strike fear in their neighbors and whet mankind's appetite anew for power and separation. Together with nation-states came a new era which has, even in the late twentieth century, insisted on ethnic identity and separateness. Still, with today's new trends toward regional trade blocs and military alliances, conveyed in a language that rests on Latin but is properly called English, the world is reinstating the Roman Empire vision of peace through unity. Assisted by new technology, it can be guided towards its goals through the window of the past.

Part One

The First Century:

A Time of Youth

I. Birth of the Roman Empire

Julius Caesar

A steady wind blew across the valley of Alba Fucens, unsettling the dust of the warm summer earth. A small flock of sheep nibbled busily at sparse blades of grass peeking out from under marble columns strewn across the ground. Lucius came walking with his flock and decided to sit amid the moss-covered ruins of an aging monument. As he rested he wondered what his future might bring. He had just turned fifteen. Italy was such a big country!

Ever mindful of his duty, he scanned the valley floor with alert eyes to see that his sheep were safe. Assured that they were accounted for, he shifted in his seat and drooped his tired head into his hands. As he did so, he spotted a shiny reflection of the midday sun hidden among the vines at his sandaled feet. Bending, he scooped at it and was rewarded with a coin. It appeared to be of bronze, a common metal for coins, but to Lucius it was a unique experience, for he had never before seen one.

Turning it over and over in his fingers, he finally focused on the inscription, but he couldn't read or even spell the words. Just as he wondered at the meaning, a voice called out, "Luci, Luci, *veni, veni.*"

"**Pater**," shouted Lucius, "look what I found." Examining the coin, his father Aulus smiled, his eyes glistening in a way Lucius had never seen them before. Squinting, he read the words on the obverse: "*DIVUS AUGUSTUS PATER.*" On the reverse was a square altar.

3

"What does it mean, pater?" "Let's sit down together, son, and I will tell you how this coin came to be here in the forum of our town. It's a long story, so let's get comfortable." They settled on a broken marble column, and Lucius sensed they would be there for some time. Aulus, as if ready to unload a burden that he had carried a lifetime, breathed a sigh of relief and began to speak. Here is the story Lucius heard....

The inscription on the coin reads: "the deified Father Augustus." Augustus was the first emperor of Rome. At the time he was crowned in 27 BC, the Roman people had just ended a period of civil wars. First one general and then another had defied the Republican government and tried to take power from the people and the Senate. In the year 60 BC, Julius Caesar, great uncle of Augustus, and two other powerful generals, Pompey and Crassus, had formed the First *Triumvirate* (rule of three). It was their plan to rule Rome and her many provinces, from Gaul, all across North Africa to Egypt and Asia Minor. That plan clashed with the republican ideal of rule by the Senate and people of Rome.

Civil War

Caesar now forced the Senate to name him consul (59 BC). To strengthen the First Triumvirate, Pompey married Caesar's daughter Julia. While Caesar led the conquest of Gaul (58-51 BC), Pompey remained in Rome. Meantime, Crassus invaded Mesopotamia (54 BC). There he waged war against the Parthians. Inexperienced troops led to the destruction of seven of his legions. Their *signa* (standards), seized in battle, would be displayed in Parthian temples for thirty-four humiliating years. Crassus himself was captured and beheaded (53 BC).

With the death of Julia in 54 BC, relations between Caesar and Pompey drifted apart. Caesar initiated a civil war (49-45 BC) in which Pompey was defeated at Pharsalus in eastern Greece in 48 BC. This was Caesar's last rival in the triumvirate. He and his party were now able to seize state power for themselves. In the process, though, Caesar was creating enemies in the Senate who would soon plot against him.

Caesar increased the Senate to 900 members, undertook building programs, built a new *forum* (Forum Juli), started agrarian reforms, redesigned the calendar and accepted the accolades of the mobs of people who had come to enjoy the spectacles of Rome. To them he offered more and more gladiatorial combats. He rewarded newly powerful families with appointments to the Senate, including non-Roman Italians and *equites* (equestrians).

The equestrians were men of wealth who had not been born into the patrician class. Caesar formed new loyalties in this class. He fashioned his rule around personal loyalty, awarding friendship with favors and power. He disregarded republican traditions and the old patrician families that held seats in the Senate.

- - - - -

The Theater of Pompey was the first stone theater built in Rome (55 BC). It was a free-standing semicircle surmounted at one end by a shrine dedicated to the goddess *Venus Victrix*. No one would think its builder guilty of excessive luxury with a shrine on the arc of the theater, and Pompey felt secure with such a theater. The elegant brick-lined rooms beneath it were perfect for private meetings and intimate discussions. Their vaulting would hush the sounds of intrigue. (The underground vaulting today houses the Ristorante di San Pancrazio, while brick apartment walls still describe the mystique of the theater's outline.)

Caesar decided to hold a meeting of senators there the morning of the Ides of March (March 15) in 44 BC. The plots and rumors of plots against him suggested he avoid the *Curia*, the Senate house where the senators ordinarily met. Still, he felt strong that morning. The Senate held many of his trusted men. The plebs had been corrupted by him through the *congiaria* (public handouts of grain), and the army made dizzy with the success of arms. What enemy would be bold enough to defy his power and popularity?

Besides, Venus Victrix was a special patroness of Rome. It was she who had protected Aeneas on his voyage westward, fleeing from the burning Troy a thousand years before. It was she who had led Aeneas to the shores of Italy. There he would marry Lavinia, found the town of Lavinium and forge a race that would host the illustrious twins, Romulus and Remus. Romulus in turn would inspire a new town, and this would blossom into the city-state of Rome. With Caesar now the unchallenged ruler of Rome and her provinces, his name and fame would some day be recalled alongside those of his famous ancestors.

These must have been his thoughts as Caesar ascended the shrine steps that morning, proud and confident of his role in Rome's destiny. Reaching the sacred summit, he felt a tugging at his *toga*. He turned, and in that moment of supreme strength he was struck down with a fury. Surrounding him, the senators stabbed him to death in an act of tyrannicide they believed was justified. The stench of death now floated down the marble steps of the sacred shrine where, but a moment before, the ruler of the Mediterranean world had just stalked defiantly. The scene was one of supreme irony-- a crimson toga lying in a heap before the statue of Venus the Victor, and nearby, a statue of Pompey. The First Triumvirate was dead.

That moment will always be important to Romans, for most thought that the senators and people of Rome would now reestablish the Republic. Instead, Caesar's death brought on another bloody civil war that lasted 13 years.

The leaders who wanted to avenge the dead Caesar formed the Second Triumvirate. They included Mark Antony, Octavian (Caesar's grandnephew) and Lepidus. Legion now attacked legion, as Romulus had once fought Remus. Eventually the Triumvirate also broke into rival factions.

The bloodletting ended finally with the sea battle of Actium, Greece, in 31 BC. Caesar's own grandnephew and heir, Octavian, stood alone as victor and avenger of his great-uncle's death. Mark Antony, who had commanded the opposing forces at Actium, fled to Egypt with Cleopatra, queen of that province and his new consort. There they took their own lives, knowing their cause was hopeless.

The victory at Actium was made possible because of Marcus Agrippa, the admiral who commanded Octavian's fleet. His strategy and tactics clearly outshone those of Mark Antony, his legions and the forces of the Egyptian client state. The fleet under Octavian and Agrippa now sailed to Alexandria to establish Roman rule there and make Egypt a province. The Nile valley would become the breadbasket that would feed Rome, her people and her legions for centuries to come. Its papyrus plants would serve to record the laws and policies, the prose and poetry of Rome and her people. They would make it possible to hand down that body of knowledge from generation to generation to our time. (Today we read of Rome by turning pages of "paper," "*papyrus.*")

The victory of Actium was a sign that the West would now rule over the world. The provinces of the East, fostered by the Greeks through the conquests of Alexander (334-323 BC), were richer and had more cities and cultural traditions than the West. The Greeks, though, had never been able to find the secret of political unity. From the days of Athens, Sparta, Corinth and Troy, unity was a missing ingredient in the Greek East.

Rome, though, had withstood her civil wars and the breakdown of republican rule. Her developing, changing provinces remained unified. The Roman world would, from this time on, reflect a partnership between these two cultures, but Rome and the West would be the dominant partner for three hundred years.

Octavian must have sailed back to Rome on a calm sea. *Mare nostrum* ("our sea," the Romans called it) touched the shores of three continents, and their citizens looked to this man for leadership and peace in a new world. Born in 63 BC, Octavian was but a teenager when his great-uncle was assassinated. Now, as he marched victoriously into the *Forum Romanum* (the Roman Forum, center of ancient Rome) in the late summer of 29 BC, he created a magnificent sight. The senators, the legions, the Vestal Virgins, the priesthood, the patrician aristocracy, the plebeians, slaves, and his closest friends and advisers wound their way up the *Via Sacra* (the Sacred Road) to the Capitoline Hill. There stood the *Capitolium*. Towering over the city, it housed the three great gods of ancient Rome. Their gilded statues cast shimmering reflections upon a torchlight crowd, the ruling elites of the West honoring the mightiest gods of the Universe. They stood just inside the *cella* (cell): Jupiter in the center, to his right Juno, and to his left Minerva.

Dedicated about 508 BC, this temple had become the center of religious worship. Before its splendid columns had come sacrifices, divinations, dedications and triumphal processions. (Its original platform still stands and may be viewed in the Palazzo dei Conservatori.) What pride filled the hearts of these men and women as they stood and witnessed the sacrifice of a bull and chanted the thanksgiving hymn to Jupiter, the father of gods and symbol of the Roman state; to his wife, Juno, who protected the family; and to Minerva, ancient Etruscan goddess of arts and crafts, who came to symbolize wisdom and the hunt.

The Age of Augustus

The greatest problem Octavian now faced was his own army. The master of seventy legions, he decided that only twenty-eight were needed for Imperial defense. The treasury, weak from the civil wars, could not support a larger army. Octavian must find land to settle more than forty legions and yet respect the property of others and not raise taxes. He solved this problem by settling the ex-soldiers in the lands of *Hispania* (Spain), *Gallia* (Gaul), Syria, Africa and Dalmatia, where recent conquests would become future provinces.

By strokes both large and small Octavian absorbed power to himself while creating a strong central government and an Imperial administrative service that could rule over an empire. On January first, 28 BC, Octavian and Agrippa became consuls. Now the Senate could be reduced from a thousand to six hundred, undoing the work of Caesar and returning its number to the figure set by Sulla earlier in the century. Octavian adopted Caesar's policy of making appointments to both the Senate and the equestrian class from among non-Roman Italians and men from the provinces of Spain and Gaul. He improved the status of the equestrian class, making equestrians salaried employees of the state in both civilian and military positions. He formed an inner circle of advisers, his "cabinet." He hired many freedmen to serve in his household. They became some of his most trusted advisers.

The title *Imperator* (emperor) had traditionally been given to a victorious commander-in-chief, to be held until his *Triumph* (victory celebration) ended. Octavian adopted it as his *praenomen* (first name). From the time of Emperor Vespasian it became the title of every emperor.

Meeting with Octavian in the Curia on January 13, 27 BC, the Senate signalled its loyalty to him by granting him the title *"Augustus"* ("Revered"). It approved all his acts, made his birthday a holiday and ordered triumphal arches at Brundisium and Rome.

The doors of the Temple of Janus slammed shut for the first time since the First Punic War had ended (241 BC). Legions would no longer have to march out of the city to war. *"Pax Romana,"* "Roman Peace," became an Augustan reality that future generations would look upon as the ideal of both the good life and orderly government.

Augustus was honored with many triumphs, yet he was not considered a great military leader. He led his final campaign into Spain (27-25 BC). There he was injured and also took ill, marking the last time he would take the field.

Successful Roman leaders traditionally led their troops to war, thus gaining the support and loyalty (*fides*) that brought prestige. Augustus was taking a calculated risk that his legions would always remain loyal to him as emperor. To ensure this, he made the army into a professional organization. He did this by screening the sons of senators and equestrians and choosing the best of them for his officers and commanders. Forming an all-volunteer army, he began training programs and set salaries for all ranks. His twenty-eight legions numbered about 180,000 men. He continued the practice of drafting non-citizens for auxiliary troops. Their numbers were set at ca. 150,000, and all were conscripts from the provinces.

Soldiers went through a basic training program. Infantrymen learned the phalanx formation, with its emphasis on mobility and flexibility. They were issued a short sword, javelin and shield and carried a field pack weighing about sixty-six pounds (similar to the weight a soldier carries today). Most soldiers were expected to serve for twenty years. They were then issued mustering-out pay and were offered land in return for their years of service.

Augustus established a special legion, called the Praetorian Guard. Consisting of the best and most loyal troops, this legion was the only one stationed in Italy. It was comprised of nine cohorts, each numbering 480 men. Its duties included guarding the emperor, the public buildings of Rome and its surroundings. Most of the Guard were stationed near Rome, the likely center of mob riots or other disturbances. The Praetorian Guards were paid double the salary of the other legions to ensure their loyalty. Even so, the commanders of the Praetorian Guards soon became the brokers in making and breaking emperors.

Intrigue and plots were part of Rome's heritage. Often a rumor or a word spoken in secret could spark a revolt. To protect themselves against intrigue, rulers married off their relatives to leading advisers and officials. Augustus had his only daughter Julia marry Agrippa when her first husband, Marcellus, died (23 BC). Two of their children, Gaius and Lucius, seemed to be the heirs apparent. Augustus, though, had two stepsons, Tiberius and Drusus. They were his second wife Livia's children from her first marriage to Tib. Claudius Nero. One by one the potential heirs died. Tiberius's younger and popular brother Drusus seemed the favorite to succeed as emperor. He died after falling from his horse while on campaign near the Elbe river in Germany (9 BC). Gaius and Lucius died unexpectedly a few years later.

Tiberius, happily married to his step-sister Vipsania, was now ordered to marry Julia, daughter of Augustus and Tiberius's own step-sister. Her second husband, Marcus Agrippa, general, admiral, architect and colleague of the emperor, had just died (12 BC). Even more boggling was the fact that Vipsania was the daughter of Agrippa by his first wife. Thus, Tiberius had been ordered to marry his own step-mother-in-law, Julia, since she had been married to Agrippa, his father-in-law. All this with the prospect of a male heir to the throne!

Augustus developed and set the governing standards of Imperial rule for all the emperors who followed him. No emperor was able to maintain the level of peace and prosperity he brought about, and no emperor exerted the same degree of moral reform as he did.

Augustus called upon the wealthy aristocracy to return to the simpler life, to avoid an excessive life-style, and to relive the ancient Roman qualities of *civilitas* (decency) and *auctoritas* (authority derived from virtue). Augustus himself ordered the restoration of all eighty-two temples in Rome. He encouraged devotion to the traditional gods who had made Rome's greatness possible. He proudly accepted the title *Pontifex Maximus* (high priest) when the Senate bestowed this position on him in 12 BC. His own modest lifestyle reflected the standards he advocated.

Although Augustus was known for bringing peace to the Empire, the Roman legions were heavily engaged in combat throughout his reign. No civil war would break the spell of peace that had descended upon Rome and Italy. Still, the legions under the command of his two stepsons, Tiberius and Drusus I, were engaged in major battles to establish the Rhine and Danube rivers as the permanent boundaries of the Empire in Europe. Drusus I, heir apparent to the Imperial throne, lost his life in combat along the Rhine in 9 BC. Tiberius fought into *Noricum* (Austria) and *Pannonia* (Hungary). Later posted to the East, he gained the honor of receiving back in 19 BC the Roman standards taken by the Parthians in 53 BC. The reluctant Tiberius would become the adopted heir by default in AD 4.

- - - - -

The riverine borders of Europe formed the Imperial division between Romanized western and barbarian eastern Europe. Their presence allowed the roads, bridges, aqueducts and drainage systems of western Europe to be built. Roman camps would slowly be transformed into the cities of England, France, Belgium, Germany, Spain and Portugal, Austria, Switzerland and Hungary.

These laid the future foundation for law and order, Christianity and the preservation of Classical learning, as well as the development of the Romance languages. Later still, nation-states would rise from the ashes of a fallen Empire, but they would be guided by the only model they had: the kings, the czars and kaisers, who drew both their titles and their visions of unity from Caesar Augustus.

Yet, tragically, the prosperity of the Pax Romana also served as the stimulus to barbarian invasions. They would place the borders of the Empire under constant attack until, by the fourth century, invasions from east of the Rhine and north of the Danube would make a blur of frontier fortresses, walls and the loyal Roman legions who fought from within and atop them.

It is small wonder, then, that the Senate voted in 13 BC to build an altar of peace to recognize all that Augustus had done for the Roman people. Known as the *Ara Pacis Augustae* (Altar of Augustan Peace), it was dedicated in 9 BC. Considered the greatest marble paneling ever sculpted, it stands about 15 feet high and has two entrances. The exterior walls are covered by an upper band with members of the Imperial family, dressed in togas, advancing in solemn procession to a sacrifice. A floral motif with swans decorates the lower band. The goddess *Roma* appears on another wall, as does *Tellus* (Mother Earth), holding on her lap two children and surrounded by the fruits of the land. Romulus and Remus at the foot of the Palatine Hill are guarded by Mars, and Aeneas is offering sacrifice to the *Penates* (household gods). Augustus is slowly taking on the trappings of a deity in the eyes of the Senate and the people. The Altar (*Ara Pacis*) is a brilliant display of world-class art. It is still standing in the *Campus Martius* (Field of Mars) near the Tiber.

Augustus also continued Caesar's work of beautifying Rome. The whole era saw the rise of lavish buildings on a scale never before witnessed. The temple of *Mars Ultor* (Mars the Avenger) is the centerpiece of the Forum of Augustus, one of the four great Imperial forums. Seventeen steps lead to the summit of the temple, where three massive Corinthian columns still stand, conveying *dignitas* (dignity, the feeling of personal worth or social honor) and *pietas* (dutifulness toward the family, the gods and the State). One departs the temple ruins with a lingering feeling of divinity itself.

The *Mausoleum Augusti* (Mausoleum of Augustus) was constructed near the Tiber in 28 BC. Built to resemble an Etruscan domed tomb (*tumulus*), it housed the Imperial family's ashes, from Augustus to Nerva (AD 98). The Temple of Apollo on the Palatine Hill, completed in 28 BC, was the first in Rome constructed entirely of white Carrara marble. On either side was a library, one for Latin books, the other for Greek. The *Pantheon* (Temple of all the gods) was designed by Marcus Agrippa, Augustus's colleague and general, in 27-25 BC. It was rebuilt as a domed temple by Hadrian in AD 136, the most inspiring engineering work of the Roman Empire. Augustus was certainly accurate in remarking before his death that he "had found Rome a city of brick and left it one of marble."

The great body of Classical literature was penned under the mantle of Augustan Peace, as well. Vergil, Horace, Ovid and Livy were some who defined "classical" stature for their timeless human expression, their fluid prose and poetic beauty. Vitruvius became famous for his treatise on architecture at the same time. And Augustus himself wrote the *Res Gestae*, a detailed treatment of his accomplishments during sixty years in politics. In it he gives an exhaustive account of all he has done in the fields of territorial expansion, law-making, building, conducting the censuses, and his moralizing goals for society.

Augustus wove the past and present into a unified tapestry of civilization which could thrive in peace and ethnic harmony. *"Festina lente"* --make haste, slowly!--was at once his favorite saying and his guideline for personal achievement.

Strangely, the most pivotal event in world history occurred during his reign, yet he would die never knowing of it. It was during the first Empire-wide census he ordered, that the Jewish *Messiah* (Redeemer) was born at Bethlehem in the province of Judaea in the year 754 a.u.c. (*ab urbe condita*, from the founding of Rome). Through the concurrence of these two great epochs, one--the Roman--would make possible the other--the Christian. Even though the two were mutually contradictory in their final goals, Christianity "found its feet" in the pagan shadow of the Roman Pantheon.

Eventually Christianity carried its message through the medium of that Empire. It traveled along the roads once trodden on by legions. It preached in the temples converted into churches. It directed the citizens in their conversion from polytheism (many gods) to monotheism, the worship of one God. And Rome herself, though she lost her Imperial crown, became the capital of the Christian tradition. The New Rome would in time surpass Augustan Rome in her moral ideal, her territorial influence and her longevity.

From another standpoint, the final collapse of the Empire never occurred, despite the "fall of Rome" in AD 476. Educated Christian monks studied and copied her theories of government, her forms of art and architecture, her history, rhetoric and epic poetry. They preserved the winter of Rome's discontent from the time of the barbarian invasions to the Middle Ages. In the medieval monasteries of Europe and the Middle East, monks dedicated a lifetime to copying all the sacred and Classical writing known to exist. Their work linked Classical learning with the intellectual curiosity of the 15th century, making possible the Renaissance of learning that followed. Rome's traditions continue to form the heart and soul of Western culture down to our time.

Augustus died on the 19th of August, the month named for him, in AD 14, at Nola in Campania, at the age of seventy-six. If he transformed Rome from a Republic to a disguised Absolutism, he did it with the realistic interests of the peoples of the Empire in mind. Nothing more could have been asked of him. Nor could the collective memory of the West ever forget him. Through his reign the Pax Romana and Pax Augustana had become identical. The most appropriate epitaph for Augustus must be that: "Augustan Absolutism made possible Western Republicanism."

II. The Julio-Claudian Emperors

Tiberius

Tiberius was the firstborn son of Livia, the third wife of Augustus. He was adopted by his stepfather Augustus in AD 4 as the designated heir. He had worked closely with the emperor during the last ten years of his reign, making possible a seamless transition upon the death of Augustus.

Tiberius received from the Senate the same *imperium* (absolute power) as his predecessor, only now it was given to Tiberius for life. Thus, Tiberius was the first to inherit the tradition of power that all future emperors would receive at the hands of an ever more-compliant Senate. Imperium had shed the appearance of reluctance as the Senate had of Republicanism.

As a member of the Claudian *gens* (family) by birth, and a Julian by adoption, Tiberius united two noble houses and at age fifty-five became the first of four Julio-Claudian emperors. In many ways Tiberius was an unwilling victim of the dynastic intrigues that would hang like a bad dream over the head of the Roman *princeps* (first citizen) for centuries.

Tiberius was first happily married to Vipsania (23 BC), daughter of the famed Agrippa, in a move orchestrated by his mother Livia in hopes that he might become the heir. That same year, though, Augustus's daughter Julia was widowed, and Agrippa quickly divorced

15

his wife to marry her. Augustus, needing to plan for the Imperial succession, adopted the first two sons of that union, Gaius and Lucius, in 17 BC.

Julia was again widowed with the death of Agrippa (12 BC), and Augustus then forced Tiberius to divorce Vipsania and marry her. It was a very unhappy marriage. Julia's highly publicized affairs led to her banishment by her father in 2 BC.

Over the course of time, Tiberius had distinguished himself as a military leader. He had commanded armies for a period of twenty-two years, following Augustus's orders, quelling uprisings and enlarging the Empire, especially in *Illyricum* and *Pannonia*-- Yugoslavia and Hungary (12-9 BC, AD 6-9)--and in Germany (9-7 BC, AD 4-6). He had been sent to the Rhine area nine times and had regained the lost standards from the Parthians while in the East. Tiberius was perhaps the most outstanding military commander to become emperor up to the time of Trajan.

Though born to one of the most aristocratic families, he did not experience happiness in his personal life. Passed over several times as the favorite to succeed to the principate, and embarrassed and disappointed by Julia, he took a ship to Rhodes in 6 BC. There, seeking relief from the court intrigues and favoritism that seemed to evade him, he studied rhetoric and Greek literature and culture. He had wanted to become a skilled speaker, yet was always a poor communicator, a quality that set him apart from the easy communicative skills of Augustus. He also shunned the games, preferring the company of scholars, writers and a more refined crowd. His self-exile ended when Augustus recalled him to Rome in AD 4.

Tiberius took great pains not to encroach upon the dignity of the old Republican institutions. A Republican and conservative at heart, he respected the Senate, attended all its meetings without pretension and avoided any offer of flattery. He dropped Augustus's advisory council of senators to show that the Senate was the supreme advisory body. Still, he formed a body of advisers among friends and specialists.

Though suspicious of others from a lifetime of experiences, Tiberius was caught up unaware in a major plot filled with intrigue and power plays. Lucius Aelius Sejanus, the prefect of the Praetorian Guard, was an ambitious man and a womanizer. He had shared the prefecture with his father, Strabo, until the latter's retirement. Six of the nine cohorts comprising the Guard had been spread throughout Italy under Augustus. Sejanus changed this, asking that they all be stationed in a single new barracks on the Viminal Hill in Rome.

Tiberius relied more and more on Sejanus as adviser and confidante. Sejanus, in turn, began instituting a reign of terror while developing a plan to make himself heir to the principate. In AD 26 Tiberius decided to withdraw from Rome to live on the island of *Capreae* (Capri). His reasons included both fear for his own safety in Rome and his inability to get along with people and especially with senators, despite his tactfulness toward them. From now on he would communicate with the Senate by letter. Because his style was unclear, the Senate was left to drift along a trail of verbal uncertainties.

Sejanus gradually acquired more power and came to view his own position as unlimited. In 29 he accused Agrippina the Younger of plotting against the emperor. She and her son Nero were banished to distant islands. Two years later Sejanus became consul, a position also held by Tiberius. Since Tiberius was residing at his villa in Capri, Sejanus wielded great influence at Rome. The Senate, though, resented his ancestry as a mere knight. He finally overplayed his hand when he asked permission to marry the emperor's widowed daughter-in-law (granddaughter?).

The Senate resented this bold power play and informed Tiberius that Sejanus was plotting against him. Tiberius, his suspicions by this time fully aroused, secretly arranged for an envoy to carry a letter to the Senate. It was read aloud in the presence of Sejanus, who was expecting good news. Instead, he was accused of plotting. He was arrested on the spot, handed over by the senators to the executioner, and that very evening was strangled.

An order of *damnatio memoriae* (removal from all records) was issued against Sejanus, a final act of retribution towards one who, like Icarus, soared too near the Imperial flame. Thus was the fate of so many sealed, both those guilty of violating the *laesa maiestas* (law of treason), as well as those tainted through guilt by association. Thus was the Praetorian Guard to strengthen its growing influence throughout the centuries.

One crumbling wall still curves about the Viminal Hill in Rome, grim reminder of a barracks that brought the Guard from the periphery to the center of power. A most fitting epitaph on its decaying surface might read: "*Quod licet Iovi non licet bovi*" ("What is permitted to Jupiter is not allowed to mere cattle").

Tiberius spent the few remaining years of his life more somber and suspicious than ever. Senators lived in dread of the *delatores* (informers), since the mere shadow of suspicion could bring upon them the full force of the treason law. It was because of this period in his life that the writers Suetonius and Tacitus branded him a ruthless tyrant.

Tiberius died on the 16th of March, AD 37, at Misenum, on the Bay of Naples, at the age of seventy-nine. He made perhaps the most conscientious attempt of all the emperors to observe the traditions of his stepfather Augustus, to respect the Senate and to administer the Empire economically and humanely. It was an Empire he defended brilliantly as a general, yet ruled reluctantly as the princeps.

Caligula

Blood lines formed the complex web that determined who would assume the role of princeps. Tiberius had left as heirs both his grandson by birth, Tiberius Gemellus, and his adoptive grandson Gaius. When Tiberius went to live on Capri, he took Gaius with him. When the plot by Sejanus was uncovered (AD 31), the latter's wife Apicata committed suicide. Before doing so, she had penned a letter to Tiberius implicating her husband in the death of Tiberius's son Drusus II. She had also named her husband as a lover of Livilla, the wife of Drusus.

Because Tiberius believed Apicata, he gradually developed a distaste for his own grandson, Gemellus. Though Gaius and Gemellus were joint heirs, the Senate acclaimed Gaius, nicknamed Caligula, as the new emperor. He was clearly favored by Tiberius and had the advantage of being the elder of the two heirs. This selection was confirmed by Quintus Macro, the new Praetorian prefect. Once installed as emperor, Caligula formally adopted Gemellus to maintain good relations.

Suetonius described Caligula as tall and pale and unsound both in body and mind. As a child in *Germania* (Germany), the legionaries of his father Germanicus fashioned a little pair of boots for him to wear, which were called "caligula." The name stuck.

Caligula came to the throne amid rising expectations. Many felt the dawn of the "New Era" had arrived as the 24-year-old rode down the Palatine Hill and across the Forum in a glistening chariot. The citizens of Rome had not seen the Imperial purple for ten long years. A hush rolled across the crowd as the new princeps came riding past the temple of Vesta and into the open space before the Senate House. All of Rome hailed the youthful Caligula, capable of expressing the grandeur of empire. This Rome needed. This the masses cherished.

Caligula was well schooled in both Greek and Latin and was considered an excellent speaker. As an adult, he slept very poorly and used to wander the palace halls at night.

He gained the support of the main sectors of society early in his reign. He reduced taxes, pardoned political offenders and was generous in support of public entertainment and donations to the city's masses. He ended the treason trials that had been common under Tiberius. He also promoted some knights to the Senate. He was, from the start, the darling of the patrician class. He seemed a welcome relief to a Senate that had existed for many years in morbid fear of the gloomy Tiberius.

In October 37 Caligula suffered from a serious illness, and some date the strangeness of his reign to that illness. He began to take extreme positions from that time on. The next year he had both Gemellus and Macro commit suicide. It was common practice in Imperial circles to offer a condemned man the option of suicide. It was the only way he could save the inheritance for his family, which included his honor, his name and his position in society, as well as his possessions.

During his short reign Caligula transformed Imperial rule into an autocracy. Senators were again forced to live in suspicion of one another. Their rights were trampled on. Excessive taxes damaged the emperor's support among the people. Early in 39 the emperor reinstated the infamous treason trials. He wished to be called *dominus* (lord) while still alive, a title reserved for emperors deified after their death. He ordered the heads cut off from the statues of the gods.

Caligula seems to have taken a Hellenistic view of life--part of his erratic childhood influences. His grandmother Antonia was the daughter of Mark Antony, who was cast under the spell of the Egyptian Cleopatra. Antonia played a small role in Caligula's youth. He was said to have lived in incest with all three of his sisters, and he married four times during his short life. Certainly incest reflected the practices of Egyptian pharaohs, who had captured his imagination.

Still, none of this quite explains the enigma that Caligula became. He had a bizarre sense of humor. While traveling through Gaul, he arranged a speaking competition in Latin and Greek. The losing orators were required to erase their speeches with their tongues.

He developed earthy tastes. Enjoying the excitement of chariot races at the *Circus Maximus* (the main race course in Imperial Rome, it dates from the sixth century BC), he became a charioteer and spent many evenings at the stables, talking and joking with the riders. He liked to portray himself as a singer and dancer, and he fought as a gladiator for pure sport in Rome's arenas.

This attention to so many leisure pursuits allowed him little time for governing. To fill the gap, he employed freedmen. Many of these were Greeks from Alexandria, who were known to be anti-Jewish. This helped gain him a reputation that was both anti-Semitic and philhellene.

Victimized finally by his own absolutism, Caligula became the first emperor to be assassinated. A tribune of the Praetorian Guard, supported by other conspirators, ended his life with a dagger on January 24th, 41. The Empire was now for the first time without an heir.

For twenty-four hours the destiny of Rome hung in the balance. Who should be heir? Should the Republic be restored through the "*Senatus populusque Romanus*"? ("The Senate and the people of Rome," abbreviated with the letters SPQR. Those letters once fluttered from every banner carried by a Roman legion. They were the very symbol of the Republic.)

The Senate broke into factions over the issue. Some wanted a return to republican government. Others, seeing that the factions could break into open warfare and destroy the Empire, favored the Principate. Still others went into hiding, lacking the ancient virtues to stand up for their beliefs. The Praetorian Guard, quick to act, found Claudius, Caligula's uncle, hiding in the palace. Taking him forcibly to their camp, they proclaimed him princeps. The next day the senators, one by one, went out to the Viminal Hill and accepted the choice of the Guard. With this, the last dreams and hopes of restoring the Republic came to an abortive halt.

Claudius

The Senate no longer had leaders, only factions. The pendulum of power had swung to the Praetorian Guard. A Republican institution-- the Senate--had surrendered leadership to an Imperial one--the Guard. Autocracy would become the rule rather than the exception for the next four centuries. The actions of the Guard would give rise to a new word, a new institution, a new practice among republican governments of the future--*praetorianism* (the interference by the military sector in the government of a republic).

Not even the most perceptive *haruspex* (diviner) could have recognized in a lamb's *iecur* (liver) that Claudius would one day become emperor. It was his older brother Germanicus who had followed in their father Drusus I's footsteps. He had distinguished himself as a military man, leading expeditions into his father's territories and making annexations in the East.

With their father's untimely death in Germany in 9 BC, Germanicus now became the adoptive brother of his uncle, Emperor Tiberius, who passed over both his own son and grandson as candidates to succeed him. (The palaces on the Palatine Hill nurtured plots as well as rumors of potential heirs to the throne.) Then, unexpectedly, Germanicus died in 19. Tiberius now looked to his own son, Drusus II, who was advancing on the *cursus honorum* (political career ladder) but had a reputation for crudeness. Still, he was well married to his first cousin Livilla, sister of Claudius and Germanicus. Unfortunately, Drusus II met death suddenly in 23, probably the victim of Sejanus's plotting. Perplexed by this time, Tiberius adopted his own grandson, Tiberius Gemellus, and his brother's grandson, Gaius (Caligula), the surviving son of the renowned Germanicus. At the death of Tiberius, the Senate rushed to the support of Caligula, and with that the Julio-Claudian dynasty had found continuity.

As mentioned earlier, Caligula met an untimely fate, assassinated at age 29 without a designated heir, after four despotic years. To underscore their disgust, his murderers searched for his wife and infant son and put to death that same night. This time it was the turn of the Praetorian Guard to select an heir, and they did so, raising from obscurity Caligula's neglected uncle Claudius, aged fifty-one.

Claudius had been the ugly duckling of dynastic plans for half a century. Though well built, he was sickly and clumsy, dragging his right leg as he walked. It was said that his voice sounded like a foghorn, and he stuttered so badly that others couldn't help laughing. His personal habits included an unrestrained weakness for wine and women.

Still, Claudius was not the imbecile others made him out to be. He was good at heart: one of his first acts was to allow Agrippina (the Younger), who would become his fourth wife and was the mother of Nero, to return from exile at Ponza. The fact that she was Claudius' brother Germanicus's daughter, and thus his own niece, simply made life on the Palatine that much more intriguing. What claims would this woman, cunning and shrewd, energetic and violent, exercise within the dynastic bedchambers? She was the sole survivor among the three daughters of Germanicus. Proud of her Claudian ancestry, she had first married Ahenobarbus, grandson of Mark Antony and Octavia. Their son Domitius (Nero), born in 37, seemed destined for stardom. There coursed through his veins the paternal genes of Julius Caesar himself, his grandniece Octavia, and her husband Mark

Antony. On his maternal side were such luminaries as her (Agrippina's) great grandmother Julia, daughter of Augustus, first divinity of the Julians. With this in mind, Agrippina would bear watching.

Claudius, progeny of the same ancestral lines, was both sensitive, intelligent and talented. He had spent his early years in reading and writing. He had written histories of *Etruria* (Etruscan Italy) and Carthage. His intellectual ability had been recognized early by Augustus. He was given excellent tutors, including the great historian Livy. He became an expert on Roman law and government, and thus was in some respects prepared for the role of princeps.

As emperor, Claudius set about immediately to bind his relations with all sectors of Roman society. A grain shortage in 42 led him to direct work on a port at Ostia, the city at the mouth of the Tiber River. A lighthouse and a canal to control the flow of the river helped secure the arrival of wheat, two-thirds of which came from Africa. He began the project to drain the Fucine Lake. With this he helped to end the annual flooding and to create rich farmland just 85 kilometers from Rome. Two great aqueducts were constructed by Claudius, namely, the *Aqua Claudia* and the *Anio Novus*. He also had Agrippa's aqueduct, the *Aqua Virgo*, repaired in 44-46. (Perhaps it, too, will achieve immortality, for it services the Fountain of Trevi.)

Claudius was, in fact, a very talented individual. He gave new direction to the administration of the Empire through long-lasting innovations and reforms. He organized the government into a hierarchy and bureaucracy. He did this by creating a Cabinet with three major positions, all headed by freedmen: a secretary of state, headed by Narcissus; a financial secretary, on whom all the procurators of the Imperial provinces would depend, headed by Pallas; and a secretary to administer all petitions, headed by Callistus. Freedmen were appointed to these powerful positions, a reflection of their backgrounds in training and service. More than anything else, though, they brought dedication to the person of the emperor. As Claudius once observed, their strong suit was loyalty and gratitude, something too few freeborn men reflected. The equestrian class was also entrusted with high positions.

With the executive branch firmly in place, unity and speed, reliability and confidence became the immediate by-products of Imperial rule. If Augustus himself had introduced the practice of employing freedmen in important positions and Caligula had found it a convenient substitute for his laziness, Claudius made it the cornerstone of Imperial administration. Still, this reorganization of the Empire came also at the expense of senatorial power. As more and more decisions were made in the palace, fewer and fewer would be made in the Curia. The pendulum of power continued to veer toward the Palatine.

Directing his attention to the Senate, Claudius required members to attend all sessions. He reviewed the finances of each member, removing those whose family fortunes no longer met the required one million sesterces. He attended senatorial sessions, and there he passed many edicts and laws, reflecting both a sense of humanity and of social strictness. To strengthen the commitment of freedmen to their masters, he ordered that a freedwoman become a slave if she married a slave without the master's knowing. He made it obligatory for masters to care for their ill slaves. If a master abandoned an ill slave in the famed temple of Aesculapius on Tiber Island, and the slave recovered, the master could no longer claim him. A mother was entitled to inherit from any of her sons who died without a will. In confiscations, property belonging to the children could no longer be taken by the state. Claudius also speeded up court cases and set maximum fees for lawyers.

Though he was greatly concerned with justice, one of the emperor's practices sent tremors of fear among senators and equestrians. This involved him in hearing cases and dispensing justice himself, "*intra cubiculum principis*"--in the privacy of his inner chambers. When Nero replaced Claudius in 54, one of his first edicts was to put an end to this hated practice, which seemed so unfair to those who were condemned by it.

As an emperor chosen by the troops, Claudius was popular with the military. Even though he had no military background, he consciously favored that sector--and the populace, as well. And they supported him, too. He clearly recognized where his strengths lay.

Suspicion was a curse which hung over the emperor as it had over Tiberius. Some 35 senators and 300 knights died during Claudius' reign, condemned through court intrigues and the fear of conspiracies. Even a mere accusation was often met with reprisals as harsh as those of actual intrigue. So great were the plots both inside and outside the government that sleeping lightly became a requirement for longevity within the Imperial palace. Claudius, then, rose to the challenges of his position, willing to appease his supporters and to check his detractors.

Not surprisingly, when the opportunity arose to send the legions to quell an uprising in southern *Britannia* (Britain), Claudius made clear his intention of leading the invasion. He set out for Britain in 43, joining the legions and leading the march to *Camulodunum* (Colchester). He remained on the island over sixteen days, returning to Rome to celebrate a triumph in 44. The military operation was so great and successful that Britain became one of six provinces added to the Empire during Claudius' reign.

In a generous mood, the Senate voted to give both Claudius and his son the name Britannicus; and to erect arches at Boulogne, France, and at Rome in his honor. Even his wife Messalina received honors. Messalina had her own set of priorities at the palace, but they conflicted with the power loop of the emperor. Thirty-four years younger than he, she was known as cruel, lusty and plotting. While the emperor was in Britain, she married one of her lovers in a public ceremony. Some time later, she was killed by Narcissus, possibly acting without orders from the emperor.

Augustus and Tiberius had wielded absolute power and disguised it as Republicanism; and Caligula had openly and wantonly used that power; it was Claudius who channeled it into a force to serve the Empire. The Imperial bureaucracy became an essential feature, fanning out from Rome. Though Augustus had first employed freedmen in the conduct of the affairs of state, Claudius raised the practice to new heights. In doing so, he blunted the ambitions of both senators and equestrians, effectively placing them under Imperial control. The patricians would from now on look to the military for leadership. Praetorianism had become the mechanism of state succession. And both the Roman bureaucracy and Praetorianism became legacies of the West when finally the Roman Empire came to an end.

As for Claudius, his last years were spent reacting to plots and living to excess. The aging glutton would eat and drink without end. He would pass out in the *triclinium* (dining room). A pair of Nubian giants would pick him up and carry him to his apartments. Sober the next morning, he would hold some private meetings in his *tablinum* (office). Soon it would be time to be carried to the Forum, there to attend the Senate meeting, write out some edicts, and then be carried back up the Palatine Hill. Once in the palace, he took care of some personal affairs, met with his counsellors and then prepared again for the evening ritual.

Claudius' evening meals always included a few guests, mostly members of the household. Agrippina was certainly the most conspicuous of these. Married to Claudius in 49, she spent the next five years grooming her son Nero for the future. During this time Nero was reared in the palace with such luminaries as Claudius' son Britannicus and General Vespasian's elder son Titus.

Agrippina also spent her time cultivating the favor of the Senate and high officials within the palace. She was, after all, the daughter of Germanicus and Agrippina (the Elder). Both had been senatorial favorites, and now their daughter lost no time nurturing the support of the movers and shakers of the Curia.

Among her first acts was to bring back Seneca, exiled to Corsica by Caligula. Seneca was to become the guru of the Palatine. Born in Cordoba, Spain, in 6 BC, he had risen through the study of Greek philosophy to enjoy the favor of the patricians at Rome. His essays and lectures on Life and Morals made him a desired guest on social occasions. Just after a lecture one day, Julia Lucilla, incestuous sister of Caligula, had pressed him for a further explanation of some point in his talk. Seneca obliged, but he sat a bit too close to his hostess in her sedan-chair. Caligula took offense and Seneca's brief career ended in banishment.

Now, after eight years, Seneca was invited back to the Palatine Hill. There he would enjoy a new lease on life. His task would be to tutor

Nero and once again approach the pillars of power. He was viewed as a paragon of the ancient virtues by the patrician class. He spoke in lofty terms about concern for the poor, though the great estate he was building up belied his sincerity. Nero could benefit highly from such a tutor. He grew visibly in elegance and the favor of the patrician classes as he progressed through the *cursus honorum* (political career ladder). Agrippina had still other objectives that Seneca would serve.

The year was 54. Claudius could only watch as his own power waned. Through physical excesses he had become ever more senile, slowly losing his administrative grip. It was time for Agrippina to act. In a conspiracy orchestrated by her, Claudius was served poisoned mushrooms at an evening dinner she attended. (Though historians dispute the fact, the evidence of deliberate poisoning seems very probable.) Claudius became violently ill and died in his bed two days later. It was a triumph for Agrippina, whether one sides with her innocence or guilt. The colorful tyranny of Claudius had ended. The Senate was relieved. The designated heir was Nero.

Nero

At the moment when the 16-year-old Nero was crowned *princeps* (first citizen), no one could have celebrated with greater gusto than his mother Agrippina. She had laid the groundwork for her son's rise to the pinnacle of power through her alliances stretching from the Palatine to the Curia. Stylish, witty and clever, Agrippina had nursed her ambitions so well that the Senate recognized her son as the new *imperator* (emperor) almost without a murmur. It had long anticipated the accession, for there was no rival.

Nero had enjoyed the comfort and advantages of the palace for five years as the adopted son of Claudius, who had made Agrippina his fourth wife. The teenage emperor was surrounded by the luxuries of his time. The palace tutors were the best to be found, and the boy found pleasure at every turn.

Nero probably looked like most Roman youth. He was thick-set, not very tall and had blue eyes with a trace of auburn in his hair. Tutored by Seneca, he was a talented teenager. He spoke Greek and loved poetry and sculpture. Like the sun-god Apollo, he played the lyre. He felt at home in the theater, listening to the poets recite their verses. Unwilling to be held entirely by the Muses of Art, Nero also thrilled to the races at the Circus Maximus. Dust, mixed with the rumble of a dozen teams of horses threatening carnage as they rounded the *metae* (end posts), and the roar of the crowd: the gripping scene, taut with suspense, held him hostage. The same was true of the poets and orators who kept him in rapt attention for hours at the theater.

Attentive to her son's future, Agrippina arranged for him to marry his adoptive sister Octavia in the year 53. Both were too young for marriage, so they simply avoided each other. The ritual marriage nevertheless seemed to guarantee Nero's future dynastic claims.

While Agrippina was tinkering at one level, Seneca and Burrus, Nero's secretary of state and Praetorian prefect, were giving strong direction to the administration of the Empire. Still, their desire for power formed a rivalry with Agrippina. Though she often checked her son's capricious behavior, his lust for life served the interests of Seneca and Burrus. They were delighted to run the government without his interference.

Nero liked to live-it-up with his friends, even as emperor. After a short time Agrippina became intolerant of his nightly expeditions into the city with his rowdy comrades. To try to keep him under her control, she showed favoritism toward his adoptive brother Britannicus, Claudius' own son. It was the kiss of death. When Nero recognized this, Britannicus was quickly poisoned. Most senators considered it justifiable homicide, but Nero developed an appetite for even more outlandish acts. He sent his mother out of the palace and off the Palatine Hill. She went to live with Antonia, probably her adoptive daughter, who was also the sister of Octavia.

Most emperors felt obliged to entertain the masses, and now it was Nero's turn. In office only a year, he sponsored a massive *venatio* (hunt), in which 400 bears and 300 lions were slaughtered. Many gladiators paid with their own lives, too, but this was Rome, decadent from the top down. Two years later (57) Nero built a wooden amphitheater, the first of its kind, in the Campus Martius, just outside the original city limits. It would become his personal stage.

Nero's private life, like the sunflower, was rotating hopelessly toward the glitter of public approval. In 58 he gave a 400-sesterce *congiarium* (dole) to each one of Rome's masses. The 200,000 unemployed, trouble-makers and sloths of the city carried a document identifying themselves as citizens, thus making distributions of grain and money orderly. Far from an inert quantity, they could sow the seeds of discord if emperors didn't offer them monthly grain and frequent spectacles. If ignored, they rioted in the streets, unnerving the police, the Guard and the emperor himself. *"Panem et Circenses,"* "bread and circuses," was both a slogan, a shout and a warning that no emperor could afford to overlook.

That the masses and slaves could express themselves is clear from an incident that occurred one evening in the year 61. Pedanius Secundus, the *praefectus urbi* (Rome's police chief), was assassinated by one of his slaves. According to an ancient law, all the slaves in the household must now die. A *senatus consultum* (a special meeting of the Senate) was held in the Curia. When the members filed out that night, one could read the verdict in their faces: the law must be upheld. A torch-bearing mob had gathered to express their disgust with the law. Though their protest rose to an uproar, one by one 400 innocent slaves were executed. The slain official had been a trusted friend of Nero's, and though the emperor personally opposed the punishment, he chose not to interfere with the outdated tradition.

Nero's lack of self-discipline gradually opened the way for his despotic rule. He fell in love with Poppaea Sabina, the charming wife of one of his drinking buddies, M.Salvius Otho. To clear the way for himself, he sent Otho to **Lusitania** (Portugal) as governor. The whole affair was upsetting, both to his advisers and his mother, Agrippina. Poppaea was the first to suggest that Nero remove Agrippina permanently, the only obstacle to his divorcing Octavia. Nero accepted this idea. First he tried poison. When it failed to work, he had the ceiling over his mother's bed rigged to collapse. That, too, failed.

This set the stage in the year 59 for one of the most famous crimes in ancient history. First, Nero organized a banquet for his mother at

Baiae, a thermal resort on the Bay of Naples, the setting for many aristocratic villas. Matricide must appear to be an accident. That night, when the dinner had ended, Agrippina boarded a ship back to Antium. With the collaboration of the freedman Anicetus, commander of the nearby fleet, her vessel had been rigged to sink. It began taking on water near Cape Misenum. Though injured in the sinking ship, Agrippina swam to shore by moonlight and reached her villa on the Lucrine lake.

Aware of the treachery, she nevertheless sent word to Nero of what had happened. Nero was now frightened, but Anicetus took charge. Taking with him a centurion and a naval captain, he reached the villa and there murdered Agrippina in cold blood.

The matricide marked a major turn in Nero's despotism. He returned to Rome only after an official version of Agrippina's death had been accepted by the Senate. His first act was to offer a prayer of thanksgiving at the Capitolium. Next, he sent his *de jure* (legal) wife Octavia into exile in Campania on charges of infidelity. The uproar in Rome could be heard across its seven hills, and Octavia was quickly returned, delighted to have the support of the people. The erratic hand of the emperor had momentarily been stayed.

The situation at the court, though, had become intolerable to both Nero and Poppaea. She suggested to the emperor that Octavia might marry again and, if supported strongly by the people, could threaten him. Another story of adultery was now floated about the city, and this time Octavia was exiled to the island of Pandataria. A few days later Praetorian Guards arrived there with a condemnation order. Octavia refused to commit suicide. The Guards seized her, gagged her and cut her wrists. Then they threw the innocent girl into a cauldron of boiling water. When their job was done, they brought her head back and presented it to Poppaea. Though cluttered with both fratricide, matricide and uxoricide, the way was now clear for Nero to marry Poppaea. And that he did.

Soon Nero's many interests intensified. He began to show increased partiality toward chariot-racing, not merely as a spectator but as a participant. The amphitheater in the Campus Martius could release water into a vast reservoir. There mock sea battles alternated with gladiatorial contests for the entertainment of Nero and his friends. His infatuation with poetry led him into voice training, to prepare himself for a public debut. Poppaea suggested he perform at the Theater of Marcellus. When the day arrived, with senators and their wives snickering at this outlandish behavior, Nero recited a poem on stage. He accompanied himself with the lyre. When it was over, he accepted the joyous applause and flowers from the audience. It would be the first of many such performances. (The Theater of Marcellus still stands, its walls too proud to surrender to the sycophantic reverberations of the Neronian legend.)

Poppaea's own fate would come within a few short years. Never a favorite with the masses, she seemed too aloof and haughty for them. Nero had been keeping himself busy racing at the Circus to the exclusion of Imperial duties. In fact, he insisted that senators and all high government officials attend his performances, probably requiring their applause, as well. They understood they ran a great risk if they failed to attend.

A major catastrophe took place on the night of the 18th of July in 64. Nero was resting at his birthplace in Anzio when couriers arrived announcing that Rome was in flames. The next day Nero, clearly upset, left by horseback for the capital. Once there, he joined the fire brigades that were fighting the blazing inferno. Tacitus (Annales, XV) wrote that his face was blackened and his hair got singed, like everybody else's. The fire had started for unknown reasons at the Circus Maximus, and it would rage across the city for nine days. When the smoke had finally cleared, ten of the fourteen city districts had been destroyed. Among the greatest losses were some of the temples dating from the time of the kings, and part of the Palatine. The Capitolium and the Forum were spared.

A rumor worked its way through the districts that Nero had started the fire. Clearly, he was not at Rome when the fire broke out. Once, during the height of the blaze, he took a brief rest at the palace. While there, he was asked to compose a poem immortalizing the fiery event. Taking his lyre, he walked out to the terrace. A man in the flaming ruins nearby saw him, and thus was born the rumor that has never died out, that he "fiddled" while Rome burned.

Nero helped pay for the rebuilding of the city with its almost 400,000 homeless. He had the Circus Maximus redone with marble *carceres* (stalls) and covered the *metae* (end posts) with gold. Thereafter, the 200,000 spectators at the races would always remember the benevolence of their emperor, Nero surmised.

Work now began on a lavish new palace, the *Domus Aurea* (Golden House). Nero extended the palace grounds to make larger gardens and had a statue of himself cast by Zenadore. Standing 120 feet high, it dwarfed everything in his new Imperial Gardens. The people simply called it the "Colossus." (The statue stood into the VII century. Its base is still visible near the Colosseum, named after the Colossus.)

The *Domus Aurea* rose between the Esquiline, the Caelian and the Palatine Hills. Filled with circular halls, apartments, galleries and fountains, it truly reflected the megalomaniac who built it. A mission was dispatched to Greece, returning with 2,000 priceless statues to adorn the Domus Aurea. Mosaics and marbles lined the walls and apartments of the residence, many of them covering the floors in exquisite black and white patterns (*tesserae*). Fountains tumbled from the upper reaches of 30-foot walls, forming pools that fascinated luxuriating visitors. According to Suetonius (<u>Nero</u> <u>Claudius</u> <u>Caesar</u>, <u>XXXI</u>), in the ceiling of the dining hall there were hidden tubes that released a spray of perfume upon the diners. (Even in ruins the Domus Aurea reflects the opulent excesses indulged in by Nero.)

Yet another problem hung around the emperor's neck like a millstone. Someone had to be blamed for the Great Fire, and the Christians were to become the scapegoats. The Christians had been known as a secretive sect in Rome since Peter had arrived there from Jerusalem and founded the community a few years before. Ill feelings had developed and lingered toward this sect, in part because of its secrecy and in part because it had a foreign, Eastern origin. It also recognized but one God and could not worship Rome's deified emperors.

Nero accused the Christians of starting the fire. It was convenient for him to manipulate public feelings and in that way regain the support of the people, while at the same time directing the blame away from himself. He ordered Christians rounded up immediately and brought them to trial with false accusations. Three thousand Christians, according to one writer, were tied to stakes and made into human torches to brighten the Imperial Gardens and the Vatican Circus, which he had built. Others were torn apart by wild dogs in his amphitheater. The public were allowed to watch the spectacle while Nero, dressed as Apollo, rode by in an ivory chariot. (It is more probable that only a few hundred Christians could have been rounded up at that time in Rome.)

Nero's barbarism had the opposite effect on the people. The aristocracy, senatorial and equestrian families were indignant at the inhumanity of their emperor. The writer Tacitus even claimed there was pity for the Christians. It was the last straw in the elites' disappointment at the extreme behavior of the emperor. Fratricide and matricide had been followed by the execution of Nero's first wife. After this uxoricide came the forced performances on stage by members of the elite. Public readings and chariot racing by the Princeps--the first citizen--were very contrary to the *dignitas* and customs of the senatorial aristocracy.

It was at this time that the trial of Paul of Tarsus got underway. Paul had been brought to Rome a prisoner and had been held under house arrest for about two years. Nero and Paul had actually met one night in Rome, and Paul had spoken of the beliefs of Christianity. Nero presided at Paul's trial but seemed unmoved by his explanation of Christian beliefs. A few nights later Paul was led out the Ostian Gate. He was executed by beheading since he was a Roman citizen. (The monastery Padri Trappisti delle Tre Fontane stands where Paul last knelt before the centurion. Tradition has it that three fountains sprang from the earth where his head bounced across the ground.)

Nero's arbitrary ways led to a major uprising against him in 65. Known as the Pisonian conspiracy, it involved senators, equestrians and even close personal friends of the emperor. Led by Senator Piso, at least 19 were condemned, including the aged Seneca and his nephew Lucan, the court poet. Nero's suspicions never let him rest after this, so that many generals and distant relatives were condemned without the benefit of trials--among them the writer Petronius and Nero's last adoptive sister, Antonia.

Nero continued to rely on Oriental freedmen to direct the Empire, both in Rome and the provinces, much to the resentment of the old patrician families. He contented himself now with writing and reciting poetry. One night, after an evening of revelry, he returned late to the palace. Poppaea complained, whereupon he kicked and beat her till the pregnant empress died. Her embalmed body was buried in the Mausoleum of Augustus. (The huge domed resting-place of the Julio-Claudians lies in an untraveled part of the city, its brick-strewn ruins overgrown with weeds and insects.)

Nero now chose to marry Statilia Messalina, who had been his mistress. Very soon another distraction came. It was a young man by the name of Sporus. The erratic Nero had him castrated and dressed in women's clothes. Then he married him. His appetites were becoming ever more weird. Suetonius writes further that the emperor dressed in lion skins and performed bestial acts upon young girls tied to marble pillars in the Imperial Gardens. He had become very superstitious, as well. If his *toga* (a Roman male's ordinary clothing) got caught on a chair or if he stumbled while entering a room, he remained in the palace that day. He had also become very fat and fleshy.

Nero had always admired Oriental culture, and so it was almost inevitable that he would eventually visit the East. When Tiridates came to Rome to receive the crown of Armenia at the hands of the emperor, Nero made it into a major event. It also made him feel more at home with the Oriental world, which was more understanding of a despotic leader than the West. He departed Rome in 66 with plans to visit Greece, Egypt and Judaea. The Jewish rebellion forced him to cancel all but the visit to Greece. He arrived there in good spirits and went from city to city, participating seriously in the "national games of Hellas." He played the lyre, recited on stage and took part in the chariot races in Corcyra, Actium, Corinth and so many other Greek cities that he received some 1,808 victory laurels and trophies from enthusiastic audiences. Once he fell from his chariot and lost the race, yet he was awarded the prize.

Aside from the Jewish rebellion, another serious rebellion had taken place in Britain in 61. Straining under Roman governmental greed, the powerful Iceni tribe revolted. When their king died, his wife,

Queen Boudicca, was prevented from ruling. She led a major revolt that resulted in the slaughter of 70,000 Roman troops and allies. Though the revolt was put down, Nero never visited the legions in Britain nor in Judaea, in a show of support. To make matters worse, while in Greece he sent condemnation orders to some of his most successful generals, with no reason other than his fear of power. This further alarmed the military leaders and sowed the seeds of discontent. Loyalty to Caesar would soon shift to local commanders, plunging Rome into civil war.

The emperor returned to Italy, entering *Napoli* (Naples) in a chariot pulled by six white horses. At Rome his parade featured 1,808 heralds, each bearing one of the trophies he had won in Greece. His entourage moved through the *Via Sacra* to the Temple of Apollo. Built by Augustus, it was dedicated to one of Nero's favorites. The emperor had fancied himself a New Sun and player of the lyre, attributes of Apollo. The folly did not end until all 1,808 trophies were placed in the private rooms and around his bed at the Domus Aurea.

In March of 68 the overweight and tired Nero traveled to Naples for a rest. There a messenger brought word of a revolt in Gaul, led by Vindex, a senator of Gallic origin. The explosive force of this revolt would bring a chain reaction that would rock the Empire and bring about Nero's final downfall. Vindex sent word to Sulpicius Galba, the Roman governor of *Hispania* (Spain), offering him the throne. Galba declared against Nero and accepted the leadership of the revolt. Then Salvius Otho, governor of *Lusitania* (Portugal), declared for Galba. He leaped at the chance to get back at Nero, who had posted him to this remote province in order to take his wife Poppaea.

Nero returned to Rome. After consulting with a few senators, he retired to the Domus Aurea to continue his poetry and music. When word reached him that Galba had declared himself emperor, he became concerned because Galba was from a leading family and held a high position. More bad news soon arrived: the African and German legions were in revolt, and each claimed the right to name an emperor. The forces of Galba were already marching on Rome.

Nero seemed to go to pieces. Meanwhile, the capital itself was suffering through a grain shortage. When a ship finally arrived from Alexandria, all expected relief. To their dismay, the ship carried only sand for use in the *arena*. (The word "arena" is the Latin word for sand.) Now shouts could be heard for "Vindex, Vindex," as the crowd turned its anger against Nero.

The scenario that followed was confusing. Nero requested that the Senate declare Galba an enemy, which it did. Confused and disoriented, he began issuing orders that weren't followed. As disloyal legions headed toward Rome, the palace was quickly abandoned and the senators scattered. The Forum, the heart and soul of Roman life, was still. One of the tribunes told the Praetorian Guard that Nero had fled. It was untrue--he was only in hiding--but it angered the Guard.

The night of June 10th, 68, was warm and still. The rumble of marching troops could be heard approaching Rome. Alone in the palace, Nero awoke. Alarmed, frightened and abandoned by all save a few old slaves, he mounted a horse and took the Salarian Road north toward the villa of a friend by the name of Phaon. A servant had been dispatched to the coast to alert the fleet that the emperor was on his way, but Nero's sailing days were over. Some senators had been informed of his flight and quickly declared him *hostis publicus* (public enemy). The Senate met and sided immediately with Galba. The Praetorian Guard quickly agreed. Soon Phaon's villa was surrounded by the Guard. Nero, sensing the end had come, drew his dagger and put it to his throat. His secretary Epaphroditus gave it a push. Nero fell to the tile floor, uttering the immortal words, "*qualis artifex pereo*" ("what an artist perishes in me"). The Julio-Claudian dynasty had come to an end. (The villa lies beyond the church of St. Agnes on the Via Nomentana in Rome.)

In the days that followed, there was great confusion and fear at the turn of events. Nero's body was cremated in the private crematorium of the Caesars. His ashes were placed in the tomb of the *Domitii* (now the Pincio Gardens). Civil war ensued, together with its inhumanity and excesses.

It is not surprising that a legend arose among the people that Nero was not dead. He had kept his popularity with the people through his large doles and personal excesses. Maybe he would return to prance upon the stage and there recite an immortal poem of his own composition, accompanying himself on the lyre. Or maybe he could stir the crowd at his own circus, as he rounded the metae and raced down the straightaway dangerously close to the *spina* (spine or center of the raceway). The legend that he lived, with its hopes and fantasies, was passed on for over half a century.

Nero's view of Imperial authority as the final judge of all good and evil had been accepted in the East and even among many in the West. Thus, the traditions and legends of his excesses have passed down through the ages and made Nero the best known of the emperors. Only Christians and Jews condemned his moral corruption.

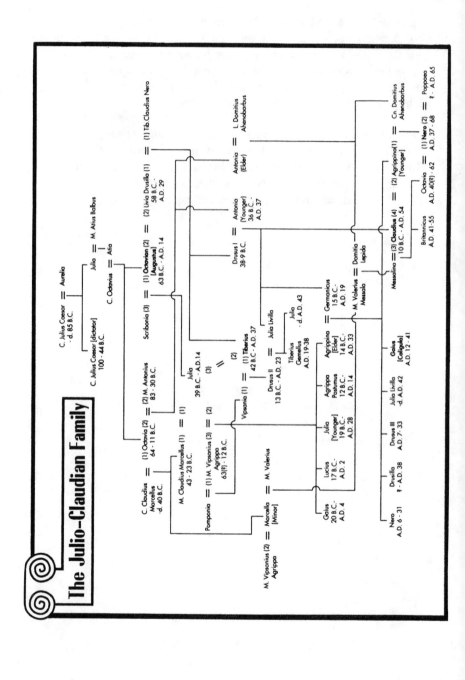

The Julio-Claudian Family

III. The Year of the Four Emperors

The Power Vacuum

Even before the death of Nero, the Roman Empire had become a broad chessboard full of ambitious men. Now at least twelve players in generals' garb were moving legions helter-skelter across the killing fields of the Mediterranean basin. Each had but one ambition: to capture the prize at Rome and keep it. Of the players, four took the city--only one could hold it.

The bloodletting that began in May 68 came mostly from the legions themselves, who fought one another as fiercely as an outside enemy. Rome and the Empire survived, but cities like Cremona were destroyed, and land and livestock, allies and opponents, friends and families, all paid a heavy price before the killing ended. Most of all, the events of 68-70 started new traditions: they showed that emperors could be made outside Rome and the Curia. They unnerved the capital by showing that frontier legions could checkmate the Praetorian Guard. They showed how important it was for an emperor to know and control his legions.

The first fires of revolt sprang up in Gaul in March 68. There Gaius Julius Vindex declared against the emperor and rallied some 100,000 volunteers to his side. He sent an appeal for support to Galba, the Roman governor of Hispania. Galba quickly declared for Vindex and began the march to Rome with but one legion. The commander of Upper Germany, Verginius Rufus, kept his legions uncommitted but

39

cut down some 20,000 Gauls supporting Vindex. With that, Vindex chose suicide as his only choice--the option of so many in his time--and the turmoil was well underway.

After gaining the support of Otho, the governor of Lusitania, and Caecina, the other Spanish governor, Galba learned of the defeat of Vindex. While pondering his next move, he received word of Nero's suicide and the Senate's support for him. Rufus now committed his seven Rhine legions to the cause of Galba. With that the road to Rome lay open to the first of three brief successors to Nero.

Galba

At age 70, Galba bore the illnesses of time. Of average height, he was bald, had a Roman nose and heavy brows. Still, he entered Rome in October 68 with a dignity reflecting his ancestral wealth and nobility. One of his first acts was to cut down a number of marines standing in formation nearby. This unnecessary act made him unpopular. There had also been many killings earlier in Spain, which left a bad taste there, adding to the worst of his growing reputation.

Once in Rome, Galba took charge with little hesitation. Orders were sent to Africa (Tunisia) and Lower Germany to have the governors, Claudius Macer and Fonteius Capito, executed. Aulus Vitellius was sent to Lower Germany to serve as the new governor. The emperor had three advisers who could not agree among themselves, a bad omen for the difficult tasks ahead.

Two new hot spots now flamed up. On January 1, 69, the army in Upper Germany (Mainz) rebelled and trampled the statues of Galba. The province of Lower Germany (Cologne) then rebelled and crowned Vitellius, Galba's recent appointment, emperor. Within twenty-four hours the seven seasoned legions of Upper and Lower Germany had united in support of Vitellius.

Learning of these events, Galba made arrangements to adopt an heir in hopes of establishing continuity at Rome. He chose a young nobleman, Piso Licinianus, a descendant of the triumvirs of Julius Caesar. This act greatly upset Otho, who had his own ambitions.

Otho, the former drinking buddy of Nero, scion of an illustrious Etruscan family, had been sent to the wilderness of Lusitania years before so that Nero could take his wife. He had been patient until his chance for vengeance had finally arrived with Vindex's rebellion. He had ridden to Rome in the same carriage as Galba. The two had campaigned together but had split only when Otho felt the sting of betrayal just once too often.

Otho now grabbed center stage. Slipping off to the Praetorian Guard, he formed a plot to overthrow Galba. Otho had good connections with the Guard. He had donated large amounts of money to the Guard and had lavished attention upon its members in hopes of maintaining good relations. By contrast, the thrifty Galba had regularly refused a donative to the Guard. He had a reputation for preferring the company of men. This, combined with his age and health, made Galba a weak figure.

Otho seized the moment to recruit some fifteen men to join in a plot to overthrow Galba. They began by spreading rumors among the Guard that they would be sent on frontier duty. On January 15 Galba and Otho attended a major sacrifice in the temple of Apollo. At a signal Otho departed and was proclaimed emperor on his way to the Praetorian camp. Galba and Piso called upon their troops to be faithful. Confusion took place among the troops in the Forum. Pushing and shoving quickly gave way to the clash of swords and a hail of spears.

As each leader mounted the *rostrum* and tried to rally troops to his side, the crowds became frenzied. Horsemen flooded into the streets and walkways, spilling about the columns of sacred temples and the walls of ancient monuments. The litter carrying Galba was dropped, and he was torn to pieces, mercifully just after his head had been severed. Mounted on a spear, it was paraded through the Praetorian camp. Piso, the designated heir, though wounded, somehow reached the temple of Vesta. One of the public slaves hid him in a private room. When a search party discovered him, he was beaten to death. That evening both men's heads were displayed from tall poles. Surely the gods of the city--Jupiter, Juno, Minerva and Janus--must have felt a twinge of regret that night at the awesome spectacle of savagery.

Otho

While Rome was in turmoil, Vitellius's armies were already en route to the capital. One such army, led by Caecina, took the short route from the upper Rhine through Switzerland, crossing the Alps through the Great St. Bernard Pass. The other, under Valens, comprised of at least 40,000 troops, was to pass through Gaul. It was a difficult trek for Valens' troops, cavalry and auxiliaries to start from Cologne in winter, follow the twisting Moselle, then the Saone and Rhone to the south of France. Passing through the territory of allies like the Treveri and Lingones was reassuring. Marching overland past walls of hostile tribes like the Mediomatrici and Aedui was unnerving, even to the seasoned legions. They panicked at Metz and slaughtered some four thousand citizens.

It was while on the march that the armies learned of Galba's death. Still they continued, eyes on the ultimate prize, moving like well-trained ants over the roads that knit an empire. Otho sent an army by sea to meet and checkmate Valens' force. The two opposing sides met in a limited engagement at Forum Julii (Frejus), near Monaco, without a clear winner. Such bloody encounters between Vitellians and Othonians would be numerous. Troops, cavalry and auxiliaries of both sides met their first major test of strength at the First Battle of Bedriacum. Fought near the Po River in northern Italy, the battle and subsequent pursuit saw the slaughter of some 40,000 men, a majority of them Othonians.

Though the soldiers truly enjoyed serving under Otho, the traditions of Rome left him no room. With his defeat at Bedriacum, he determined that the cost of war would be repeated too often for the good of the Empire. Courageously, he addressed his troops at Brixellum, not far from the battle site. Early the next morning he fell on his sword. It was the ninety-fifth day of his reign. The glories and setbacks seemed to melt into nothing as Otho was lowered into a modest marble tomb at Brixellum, but thirty-seven years of age.

Vitellius

Vitellius was leading a third army to Italy when news arrived of Otho's death. Continuing his march southward, he finally reached the outskirts of Rome. Entering the Via Triumphalis from the Mulvian Bridge, he proceeded to the city gates. It was a warm summer day. The crowds cheered as they witnessed the third great emperor to enter the Forum that year.

Born in 15, Vitellius had enjoyed positions in the priesthood and high state offices, including a consulship under Claudius when he was only 32. He had spent time at Capri as a youth among the friends of Tiberius. He had become friendly with Caligula because both shared a love of chariot-racing. An attraction for dice brought him to Claudius' attention. He got into Nero's favor because he liked the theatre. His star was destined to shine on, like Venus in a March sky.

Appointed governor of Africa in 60, he ruled with great honesty, according to Suetonius. This record was tarnished by the time Vitellius reached his new command in Lower Germany, according to Tacitus. Yet it is hardly correct. Within a mere month of his arrival at Cologne, the seven Rhine legions declared him emperor, rejecting Galba, the very patron who had commissioned Vitellius.

Vitellius would reflect some of the best and worst traits of an emperor. He revolutionized the Imperial civil service by appointing equestrians to the secretaryships. These were powerful positions that only freedmen had held before. The secretaryships had developed from the households of the aristocracy, where educated Greek slaves first served as treasurers of their estates. The private household of Augustus had developed into the first Imperial civil service. The notion of serving did not appeal to the men of senatorial rank, but the equestrian class saw how these Imperial positions had become very influential.

Vitellius also had a son, which seemed to offer the prospect of a stable change of power. During his brief period as emperor, he allowed the Senate great freedom of speech. He offered public entertainments to please the masses, and his sacrifices to the memory of Nero pleased the Eastern provinces.

One of Vitellius's first acts was to order a great feast for his army. Food and drink were his weakness, and before the banquet had ended, the rowdy troops had turned on the ever-present crowds and butchered a large number of them.

Though Vitellius had his successes, the Empire was not yet ready for peace. In the East the governors of Syria and Judaea each commanded three legions and many auxiliary forces. The commander in Judaea, T. Flavius Vespasianus--Vespasian-- was born in AD 9 in the Sabine country near Rome. Though his father was a tax-collector, he managed to get a start on the lower level of the *cursus honorum* through skill and ambition. After duty in Cyrene and Crete, he was assigned *praetor* (judge) in Rome. His first legionary command had come when he was sent to Germany under Claudius. His military brilliance stood out in Britain, where he fought in thirty battles during the great invasion under Claudius. He was awarded with two priesthoods and a consulship in 51.

When Nero became emperor in 54, Vespasian lost favor with the court, thanks to Agrippina. The emperor's mother took vengeance on anyone who had been friendly to Narcissus, her old enemy at the court of Claudius.

Shortly after Agrippina's death in 63, Vespasian was recalled from his Sabine farm by Nero and sent as proconsul to Africa. From there he was invited to accompany Nero on his tour of Greece. There he made the regrettable mistake of falling asleep at one of the emperor's recitals. He returned to his farm, eclipsed, like Venus, by the Neronic rays of morning light--until the revolt in Judaea in 67. It seemed that Nero remembered the distinguished military commander in that moment of destiny and plucked him from obscurity. He was asked to put down the revolt in Judaea at once.

At the time Vitellius claimed the throne, Vespasian commanded three legions in Judaea, and Mucianus, the governor of Syria, commanded three of his own. Another two legions occupied Egypt, the granary that fed Rome. Three client kings of the Fertile Crescent added to the Empire's might in the East.

By the middle of July all eight legions, not to be upstaged by the

European provinces, had revolted and committed to Vespasian. A great council was then held in Beirut to determine the best preparations for an assault on Italy. Routes were established, arms were manufactured, and hand-picked veterans were given marching orders.

Mucianus would lead the invasionary force across Macedonia on the Via Egnatia to the Dalmatian coast. From there ships would transport his troops to Brundisium or one of the other harbors on the southeast coast of Italy. Vespasian would remain in Alexandria to hold back the grain supply and starve Rome. His son Titus would continue the war in Judaea. Even the Black Sea fleet was to participate, guarding the flanks in Asia Minor.

As word spread westward of the challenge from the East, the five legions of Pannonia and Moesia and one in Dalmatia declared their allegiance to Vespasian. Before Mucianus could cut through Macedonia, Antonius Primus, a bold and impulsive commander, led these legions on an impromptu strike at Rome. Rushing across the Danube River plain and through mountain passes, he reached northern Italy by September. Casting aside Augustus's advice, *"Festina lente"* (make haste, slowly!), he rode the wind to reach Rome before Mucianus. It became a rivalry all its own, carrying with it all the hatred and envy that only a proud and unrefined military society could nurture.

Emperor Vitellius kept his legions in a state of high alert at Rome. He dispatched his leading general, Valens, to march northward, join Caecina, another capable general, and go in hot pursuit of Antonius. Valens followed the route up the Via Flaminia and across the Apennines. Unknown to Valens, Caecina had betrayed the emperor. Tacking to the strongest wind, he had defected to Vespasian. Luckily, the legions under his command had remained faithful to the emperor. Meanwhile, Vitellius was informed of the revolt of the fleet at Ravenna. Proceeding to the Forum, he stood before his forces and called upon them to remain faithful to the gods and traditions of the capital.

It was a courageous scene, for it came just as the legions of the Empire were preparing for a titanic engagement at Cremona in northern Italy. As the sun shed its light across the rolling plains, the forces of East and West met each other in a hail of darts and arrows, with heavily armed infantry advancing, brother against brother, in a clash of steel spears and short swords, while cohorts of cavalry, a cross-section of ethnic tribesmen shouting in a babel of tongues, rode directly at one another, jabbing and parrying, screaming and groaning, in an ebb and flow that breathed life into the profession of death itself.

When it had ended, eight Vitellian legions were strewn about in disorderly array across fields once ripe with grain, their stems now crushed and stained in crimson. Buzzards swooped down from low-lying hills while curiosity-hunters from nearby hamlets wandered amid the human waste. Antonius had won a victory; Rome had slipped from dignity; the Empire had lost its unity.

Vitellius determined to set out from Rome with fresh legions. Accompanied by senators and numerous retainers, he soon returned full circle, unable to meet his adversaries, the Vespasians. Only then did he learn of the defection of the home fleet at Misenum. He found also that Valens, avoiding the carnage at Cremona, had traveled to Gaul to recruit aid. He was captured by troops loyal to the emperor and was beheaded at Urbinum in central Italy.

By now both Antonius and Mucianus were making peace offers to Vitellius. His troops were extraordinarily loyal and begged him not to yield. Vitellius, seeing no alternative, announced his resignation, abandoned the palace, and walked with his wife and son through the Via Sacra. The crowd and soldiers blocked all the streets, demanding that he return. Again, he had no choice but to yield to their hopes.

This turn of events led to further bloodshed. T. Flavius Sabinus, prefect of the Urban Guard and brother of the challenger Vespasian, had been loyal to the emperor. Having discussed with some senators and elites the possibility of their taking the oath of allegiance to Vespasian, he found himself in an uneasy situation with the crowd and legions still loyal to Vitellius. A skirmish ensued between the two sides, and Sabinus retreated up the Capitoline Hill, the Vitellians in hot pursuit. They laid siege to the hill, where Domitian, the very son of the would-be emperor Vespasian, had also fled for his life.

In the onslaught Sabinus was captured and torn to shreds by the mob. Domitian escaped, only to become emperor himself one day. The Capitolium, domicile of Rome's three greatest deities, together with its priceless statues and furnishings, was destroyed by fire.

As the flaming Capitolium lit up the night sky, the scene must have struck fear into the approaching legions of Antonius Primus. Invading the city at dawn, they inched their way down the Via Flaminium and Via Salaria in house-to-house combat. Relentless in pursuit of their objective, they surged forward with overpowering numbers and weapons. Crowds of onlookers ranted and raved as first one side, then the other, gained an advantage. The Praetorian Guards offered the stiffest resistance, but they, too, were silenced in making a last stand at their barracks on the Quirinal Hill.

Vitellius, unwilling to escape, was taken from the palace by the Flavian tribune. With hands tied behind him, he was driven through the streets to the *Gemoniae* (the Stairs of Groans), just beyond the Forum. Humbled and spat upon, he was finally beaten to death.

So ended the quest for domination of the known world's most enduring empire. The Senate recognized Vespasian, still interdicting the grain supply at Alexandria, as the new Caesar. His son Domitian came forth to represent him, occupying the palace with his retinue.

All the Roman legions except those in Britain had participated in the civil war. As a result, the empire's frontiers had been considerably frayed during the year and a half of neglect. The spirit of nationalism, always present among subject peoples, had come alive among the Germanic tribes. Moesia and Judaea had revolted and were being checked. Julius Civilis, a Batavian chieftain, had organized a major revolt among the Germanic tribes on both sides of the Rhine river, winning the support of two legions of the Rhine army. The Celtic tribes of Belgium and northeastern Gaul also rebelled. Theirs was a less serious uprising, as most of the other Gallic tribes remained faithful to Rome.

It would take a strong and decisive hand to stay the course of empire. The shadow of Vespasian might be the last hope to cast a spell of unity upon the disparate forces unleashed by the clash of arms.

IV. The Flavian Dynasty

Though Vespasian would not arrive at Rome until the autumn of 70, the military forces had to be brought under control quickly. The troops of Antonius Primus went on a four-day rampage in Rome. Those same legions had committed unnecessary atrocities at Cremona. Primus was blamed for having encouraged Julius Civilis to revolt against Vitellius. This was at first advantageous to Vespasian as challenger, but Civilis then bolted to the cause of German nationalism, threatening the entire Roman presence in northern Europe. Primus also claimed he had won the civil war.

When Mucianus reached Rome a few weeks later, he immediately checked the claims of Primus, who took his grievances to Alexandria. There he was courteously received by Vespasian. In the end, he returned to his native town of Tolosa in France, retiring the sword that had cut a major path for the Flavian dynasty.

Mucianus was himself a colorful and noteworthy commander. Wealthy and effeminate, he presented a complete contrast to Vespasian. Energetic though self-indulgent, he was both libertine and successful administrator. He had authored a book on geography and would serve an important supporting role to Vespasian, including three consulships, until his death in 75 or 77. It was Mucianus who steadied Rome until the arrival of Vespasian. After reducing the Praetorian Guard, he dispatched his general, Cerealis, to quell the German revolt.

Meanwhile, Vespasian, departing from Alexandria with his legions, visited several cities before reaching Rome in the autumn of 70. Squarely and powerfully built, he was known as a soldier's soldier. Whether marching at the head of his army or eating rations with the infantry, he identified with the military. He knew the provinces well and recognized the security concerns of the Empire.

The Rule of Vespasian

Vespasian was the ideal *princeps* (first citizen) for Rome at this pivotal moment of destiny. Born T. Flavius Vespasianus at Reate in central Italy in AD 9, he was raised in an equestrian family. His father was a tax-collector, his uncle a senator. Though there were many more illustrious sons of the equestrians, Vespasian was a friend of Claudius' freedman Narcissus and his chief adviser Lucius Vitellius, father of the emperor Vitellius.

Vespasian began his career in the military and soon got appointed *quaestor*, where he worked on legal or financial matters in Cyrene and Crete. Moving up the *cursus honorum*, he became *aedile* (officer in charge of streets and other public property) and then *praetor* (judge) at Rome. His inspired military leadership during the Claudian invasion of Britain won him high marks, and soon he found himself governor of Africa. In February 67 he was assigned by Nero to end the bloody First Jewish Revolt. By June 68 Vespasian had limited the revolt to Jerusalem and several outlying fortresses.

When news of Nero's death reached him, he began to lay the groundwork to seize the principate. Mucianus in Syria and Tiberius Julius Alexander, the Jewish prefect of Egypt, threw him their support. In July 68 he was proclaimed emperor by the seven legions in the East, in a wave of spontaneity that sent shockwaves across the Mediterranean.

Some historians have claimed that Vespasian was pushed by the armies into becoming emperor only after the bumbling of Vitellius. Tacitus argues that Vespasian and the Eastern governors had begun their plans much earlier. Perhaps we'll never know.... Primus, commander of one of the Danubian legions, led his forces into Italy, won the second battle of Bedriacum and entered Rome the night of December 19th in 69. After Vitellius was terminated by his troops, the Senate declared Vespasian the new princeps.

Though bald and wrinkled at age 60, Vespasian showed uncommon energy and efficiency at a time when rebuilding and reconciling were major concerns. He was good-natured and enjoyed telling jokes, often the crudely obscene kind. When he spoke, one could recognize a peasant's accent, reflecting his lower social origins. He was bilingual, well read in Latin and Greek and spoke and told jokes in both languages. There is a picture of him carrying away trash on his shoulders from the Capitolium. Such was his rugged reputation. He did little drinking compared to his predecessors. His wife, Flavia Domitilla, died before he became emperor. He then lived with Caenis, a freedwoman who later became rich and powerful. After her death he had various concubines.

Upon taking command in Rome, Vespasian displayed the vision needed to place the sectors of society into a better social balance and reassure financial stability. One of his first acts was to take the name of Caesar, as the previous three emperors had done. From then on, it became the prerogative of each ruling princeps to carry the name Caesar.

Vespasian's first order of business was the army. He removed those legions that had supported the rebellion among the Germans and Gauls. Both national movements had collapsed with the arrival of fresh legions in the spring of 70. After restoring eight legions to the Rhine, he created two new military provinces in Upper and Lower Germany. The headwaters of the Rhine-Danube basin formed a dangerous gap in defenses. To remedy this, he annexed the triangle, called the *Agri Decumates* (today the Schwarzwald and Odenwald in southwestern Germany).

In recruiting new legionary and auxiliary forces on the frontier, he transferred them to different regions and placed Italian, instead of native commanders, over auxiliary troops. To further reduce the danger of uprisings, he broke up the large legionary camps into small units and spread them along the Rhine-Danube frontier. With the decline in popularity of the military career, he sent recruiters to Spain and Gaul. This stimulated the rise of *collegia iuvenum* (military academies) for the training of future officers in those provinces.

In summary, Vespasian stuck to a fair and firm policy with the military. He reconciled the legions, the auxiliaries and the commanders. He brought new ethnic groups into military service and thinned out tribal concentrations. He gave the military a new sense of direction and made his Imperial command acceptable to them. It was, after all, in his interest, since he owed them his job.

The urgencies of the Empire allowed Vespasian no rest. Fortunately for him, his elder son Titus became his efficient *alter ego* (other self). He made Titus the sole Praetorian prefect, where he was able to check plots before they became serious. He was also appointed co-consul with his father, who consciously groomed his son to perpetuate the Flavian dynasty.

One of the most compelling domestic problems lay with the Senate. That body had long since lost its independence, and it was no longer the playmaker in the game of politics. Yet, even while the Senate tended to look down upon him, he needed it as a public relations tool. To Vespasian it was of major importance to balance its sensitivities. He attended the Senate and consulted with it on all matters of state. The Senate still represented the educated class, whose opposition could spawn plots. Vespasian allowed freedom of expression in the Curia, but his vision would take him beyond the present make-up of that body.

Like Vitellius before him, the emperor began to appoint equestrians to the Imperial secretariat, replacing the freedmen who had been the "apple of discord" to both senators and equestrians. He appointed them fiscal procurators in all the provinces, including Egypt, where no senator was allowed to travel. Everywhere equestrians were sent out to man every post in the Imperial bureaucracy, with the exception of provincial governor. Senators retained the exclusive right to that position. The Senate also kept its judicial authority, but overall, it had no other effective role in government. Like an antiqued chair, it could be useful, but it served chiefly as a moral blip on the large screen of presumed continuity with the past.

In 73 Vespasian and Titus risked senatorial displeasure by taking the office of *censor*. Only Claudius among previous emperors had taken this title, and he had used it more subtly than Vespasian would. With this position, the princeps had authority to bring the lists of taxpayers up-to-date throughout the Empire. This was the best way he saw to balance the Imperial budget. It also enabled him to enroll new members in the Senate.

This was just what Vespasian had in mind. He now had the opportunity to appoint equestrians to the Senate in a serious way, raising its depleted numbers from two hundred to a thousand. Many provincials were now appointed senators. Though most were from Italy, many new ones came from Baetica in southwestern Spain, and southern Gaul, with some easterners. These new appointments meant that regional aristocracies were now serving the Imperial bureaucracy. The new policy tied local interests in with the good of the Empire, making it easier to tighten control over the provinces. It made the bureaucracy more Italian and more municipal, as many equestrians were selected from the smaller cities of Italy, as well as from the other provinces. The Senate thus became more responsive to the emperor and formed a larger body of skilled men who could serve the Empire. Above all, non-Italians made the Senate less aristocratic and more mercantile and cosmopolitan in outlook, its members expert on their regional foreign affairs. Their wealth made them more immune to graft and embezzlement. Only thirty senators still claimed ancestry to the great patrician families of the Republic. It was also very clear to some that a Senate, weakened in its independence of thought, meant a bureaucracy strengthened in its Imperial cohesiveness.

Domestic concerns were becoming ever more intertwined with foreign affairs, as the Senate and the larger bureaucracy filled with men who were experts in the affairs of their provinces. *Senatus populusque Romanus* was becoming a cliche. Aristocratic eccentricities were fading. *Dignitas* began to reflect a whole new set of Empire-wide responsibilities, from grain supply, roads and bridges, to public buildings, fleets and border security. Yet this was only the beginning of a fresh era.

One of Vespasian's major accomplishments was restoring sound finances to the Empire. He had to pay the legions, rebuild the northern Italian towns like Cremona, as well as many of the frontier camps. New roads and bridges were in constant demand. Even Rome had some damaged areas. Vespasian's solution was to increase taxes. From the census of 73 he concluded the provinces had the resources to afford more taxes without difficulty. Some "free" cities were returned to taxable status. The entire province of Greece was returned to tax-paying status. The emperor himself made a personal monopoly of pepper and started manufacturing perfumes. These funds probably helped pay for palace expenses.

Vespasian was not known for personal extravagance. He was a frugal man who took a daily drive and afternoon nap, rather prosaic by Julio-Claudian standards. Nor was personal security a major issue with him. No longer were visitors searched. He made himself available to all at his favorite spot, the Gardens of Sallust.

Despite his conservatism, the emperor still spent freely. He did not tolerate misuse of public funds. His excellent relations with the military made it unnecessary to buy legions with donatives. He saw to the defense needs, the roads, bridges and public buildings. He searched everywhere for revenue, even taxing the public urinals of Rome. When Titus came to him complaining about this extreme measure, Vespasian pulled out some gold coins, ran them by his son's nose, and asked if he thought they sent up a bad odor. (Rome's urinals are still referred to as "Vespasiani"!)

Public buildings were the visual legacy of Vespasian's rule. The *princeps* first chose to restore the Temple of Jupiter on the Capitoline Hill. Known as the Capitolium, it had been copied in every *municipium* (town) established by the Romans. The original Capitolium had been dedicated at the birth of the Republic in 508 B.C. A labor force was now set to the task of rebuilding this sacred edifice, together with copying the thousands of bronze tablets on which were recorded the laws and treaties of the Roman people. It was completed in 71.

Vespasian had planned to celebrate the victory of Titus over the Jews. He envisioned a triumphal arch, which took form as the Arch of Titus, a magnificent monument to Imperial domination. Standing at the west end of the Forum, it carries details of the triumphal parade in which the seven-branched candlestick, the table of the shewbread and other treasures from the temple at Jerusalem were displayed.

Vespasian also wanted to erect a temple to the goddess of Peace to commemorate the end of the Jewish War. He saw himself as the new Augustus, restoring tranquillity and peace. He felt also that the eyes of the Empire were focused on him. The new temple was completed in 75. Set in the Forum of Vespasian, it was a major show-place of Rome. (It is no longer standing.) The Temple of Claudius had set on the Caelian Hill for years unattended. Vespasian also had it completed.

Greatest of all his architectural pieces was the *Amphitheatrum Flavium* (the Flavian Amphitheater, now known as the Colosseum). He ordered it built on a site chosen by Augustus for a similar purpose, the amusement of the people. Yet, it was Titus who would open the yet incomplete three-storied amphitheater in 79 with a hundred days of revelry. It still stands, an enduring monument to Roman ingenuity and engineering, if not also to the collective memory of its barbaric entertainments.

The provincial policies of Vespasian also bore monumental fruits. By extending "Latin Rights" to ca. 350 cities and towns of Spain, he brought those people closer to outright citizenship. This meant so much to outsiders like the Danubian provinces of Pannonia and Moesia, which were among the last to receive Roman citizen colonies. Colonies were small garrisons, limited to 300 families. They were placed in strategic frontier locations, but lacking natural resources, they never developed beyond their limited purposes. The personnel kept full Roman citizenship. Another kind of colony, dating, like the first, from 338 B.C., often numbered 3,000 citizens. These formed the foundation of future cities.

Vespasian was also known for using public funds to assist poets and other writers. So concerned with the use of language was he that he endowed Chairs of Greek and Latin in the Imperial City. Tacitus wrote that he alone among emperors got better instead of worse as time went by. This was made possible by the helping hand of his son Titus, who co-ruled with his father in many positions.

Vespasian was the first Roman emperor of equestrian origins. He served the Empire well, balancing the budget, strengthening the military sector, building roads and monuments, encouraging education and providing for the future on a sound and organized basis. He truly had an Empire-wide view of problems. His rule shifted the history of Rome from palace affairs to the affairs of a shared civilization.

Vespasian died on 23 June of 79, at Aquae Cutiliae (Bagni di Paterno), not far from his ancestral home. He had been bathing in the cold waters and caught a stomach chill. The "second founder of the Principate" was promptly deified.

Titus: The Alter Ego

The dynasty that Vespasian had hoped to establish became a reality the next day, when Titus was proclaimed emperor. The transition from father to son was as seamless as that between Augustus and Tiberius. Titus had the experience, intelligence and charm to continue in the very footsteps of his father.

Groomed at court as a boy, he was at home among the elites, receiving the best education that the court tutors could offer. He enjoyed a childhood friendship with Claudius' son Britannicus; he knew both Claudius, Nero and their advisers. As a young commander in Judaea, he gained military experience. Finally, as his father's *alter ego* (other self), Titus had been entrusted with diplomatic missions and consulships and was appointed to the all-important position of Praetorian Prefect.

He began his short-lived principate with a full treasury. Surrounding himself with some new counsellors, together with some of his father's, he followed the general policies of Vespasian: to consolidate the Empire. His father had conquered Cappadocia-Galatia, making it a province. A network of roads was begun, continued now by Titus. His father had appointed senators from the Greek East as assistants (*iuridici*) to the governors of the new province. He had also given some of them military command. Titus confirmed their appointments. It is probable that he himself recommended these changes as his father's adviser.

He advanced the road-building program into Armenia and Mesopotamia at a time when the Parthian frontier was peaceful. With the roads came commerce and a flow of ideas. Above all, they paved the way for future expansion under Emperor Trajan. Other roads brought to completion were the Via Nova in Spain and the Via Flavia, from Trieste to Polla in Italy.

Titus advanced his father's foreign policies. The work of closing the Rhine-Danube river gap was furthered by a line of forts built with stone to better protect the legions stationed there. The new emperor founded colonies like Doclea in Dalmatia, extending Roman influence ever farther from the capital.

Granting citizenship to distant towns was also important in furthering state interests. This created unity and a vested interest in the common welfare. It also extended Rome's taxable wealth. Greek senators, appointed earlier by Vespasian, gained experience and confidence. By extending Roman influence through Hellenic officials, the Flavians laid the groundwork for the future division of the Empire into eastern and western branches.

Titus proved to be a firm supporter of the army and a faithful executor of Roman practices. He granted the military the right to make wills while still legionaries. He eased some rules on land ownership and marriage for them, as well. Sometime between 75 and 79 he fell in love with Berenice, the Jewish sister of the client-king of Judaea, M. Julius Agrippa II. The people of Rome were ever suspicious of an eastern queen--shades of Cleopatra!--and so Titus was obliged to order her to leave the city. She would return once during his reign, but once again he would send her off.

Like his father, Titus saw the importance of building. He repaired two Roman aqueducts and important roads like the Via Aurelia and Via Flaminia. He continued work on the Flavian Amphitheater, begun by his father, probably adding the third and fourth levels, as well as seating for the first two tiers. He then offered a 100-day festival for the people. It included wild beast hunts, naval battles on an artificial lake, and armies, fighting for the sheer drama and destruction of it.

This was Rome, in all its vitality, opulence and decadence. And with Rome as the model, colosseums spread across the Mediterranean, from west to east, even into the far reaches of Arabia, Africa, Mesopotamia and Asia Minor.

One of the worst disasters in Rome's history came on August 24, in the year 79, with the eruption of Mt. Vesuvius. Located just off the southwest coast near Naples, the volcano had smoldered for days when, suddenly, without warning, it exploded, hurtling into the night sky poisonous gases, fiery smoke and tons of hot magma. An earthquake followed in the port of Naples. When the eruption had spent itself, the mountainside was covered with a thick layer of ash and lava, sealing the entire cities of Pompeii, Herculaneum and Stabiae into the face of the earth.

When word of the disaster reached Rome, Titus ordered immediate assistance. Forming an *ad hoc* (for this purpose) committee--the curators for the restoration of Campania (*curatores restituendae Campaniae*)--he charged it with the task of rebuilding the scorched countryside of Campania. To finance this, he showed a shrewdness comparable to that of his tight-fisted father. He simply sold off the property of those who had died without leaving a will or heirs. This was in line with the *Lex Julia* (Julian law) of Augustus. The property (*bona vacantia*) of those who had died without wills or heirs was to go to the *aerarium*. That treasury was under strict senatorial authority. The lines between the aerarium and the *fiscus* (imperial treasury) had been blurred for a long time. Titus, facing an emergency, created revenue through sale of this property and used it as disaster relief funds, unconcerned with legal niceties.

This disaster was followed by a famine that also required emergency measures. If that were not enough, a fire swept Rome in 80, while Titus was inspecting Campania. Burning for three days and nights, it destroyed or damaged the Capitolium, the Pantheon and other state buildings. Once again both temples were rebuilt, matching or exceeding their earlier splendor. The costs of such repairs--to temples, roads and aqueducts--were borne by the state but shared also by private donors. Many times they were wealthy friends, tapped by the emperor for a contribution.

Titus lived in an exciting period of the Empire. He was shrewd and efficient and well-liked by all sectors of society. He was adept in administrative affairs, proper in society, expert in weapons and horsemanship and a composer of speeches and poetry in both Latin and Greek. He even played the harp. By all accounts he was a vigorous and effective ruler. His immortal words, *"perdidi diem"*--"I have lost a day"--were spoken upon reclining one night without being able to recall having done a good deed that day.

In September of 81 Titus set out for his beloved Sabine homeland in search of rest. He caught a fever along the way and was unable to recover from its raging effects. He died on September 13th at his father's country estate at Reate, unwittingly imitating even in death the mentor of his life, his father.

He was promptly deified, beloved by all but the Jews, who loathed him for putting down their revolt, destroying the temple of Jahweh and exiling the survivors.

Domitian: Reflections of Augustus

Titus' younger brother Domitian was acclaimed emperor without disruption of the lines of authority. Born at Rome on 24 October of 51, he was cut from a different stripe of the Flavian cloak. Assertive and ambitious, he never had the sympathy or trust of Titus and often tried to undermine him. He was also ill-humored and had a temper.

Domitian's youth led to some of his introverted ways. He had received an elite education at Rome, though it was not at court, as was Titus'. He was fluent in both Latin and Greek. This was reflected in his poetry and speeches. He spent much of his time in the inward pursuit of poetry and Greek culture. He adopted as patroness Minerva, goddess of literature. He also dabbled in astrology, not unusual for youths at that time. He used to take long walks, probably dreaming, like other Roman teenagers, about glory in war.

He never got to know Titus, eleven years his senior, or his father. Both were constantly on assignment for emperors Claudius or Nero.

Vespasian never gave him any real power. Perhaps this increased his craving for power and glory in war.

At age 18, while he was at Rome under the care of his uncle, Sabinus III, the civil war roared through the city. Taking refuge on the Capitoline Hill, he narrowly escaped death. He was protected, according to some early writers, disguising himself as a priest and joining a procession to Isis, the Egyptian counterpart of Minerva. This confirmed his patronage with Minerva and also created a strong bond between himself and Jupiter.

When Vespasian's forces entered Rome in 69, Domitian took up residence at the royal palace and was appointed praetor with consular power by Mucianus. He addressed the Senate officially on behalf of his father. He would continue in the role of balancing the Senate's desires with those of his absent father. During his father's reign, Domitian was given honors but no great responsibility. He was appointed to suffect (partial term) consulships six times, but an ordinary consulship only once. These appointments, together with various priesthoods, afforded him the opportunity to learn something about Imperial administration and also to do some networking.

He married his mistress, Domitia Longina, the daughter of Corbulo, an outstanding general who became one of Nero's victims. They had a son, but he died young, a frequent occurrence in households of that early period. Domitian stood up to his father in rejecting a dynastic marriage proposal to Titus' daughter Julia.

When news of Titus' death reached the Senate, that body met and deified him at once. Meanwhile, Domitian, hearing of his brother's illness, had gone to the Praetorian camp, and there, after promising a donative, was hailed as emperor. Only the next day did the Senate grant *imperium* to Domitian, foreshadowing the rocky relationship the two rival powers would enjoy.

Domitian, who had never been part of his father's power loop, was now *princeps*. His aim was to be a pre-eminent ruler, casting his own shadow over the Senate, the army and the people of the Empire. He would confine his reading to the entire record of Tiberius's reign. He much admired the man and saw himself in Tiberius. That ruler had not been the first choice as heir to Augustus. He had spent much time alone, profiting from his rejection by the emperor. After military successes, he had gone to Rhodes to study rhetoric. Domitian saw himself in much the same way. Toward the end of his reign, Tiberius retired to Capri. Domitian would enjoy his villa outside Rome.

Shortly after becoming emperor, he divorced or, more likely, exiled Domitia because of a scandal in which she had allegedly had an affair with Paris, a famous pantomime (*pantomimus*). He then allowed his niece Julia to remain in the palace after executing her husband, Sabinus IV, for state reasons. Whether Domitia ever had an affair with Paris or just admired him too much to keep the Imperial court (*aula*) silent, will never be known. But Domitian now faced another dilemma--rumors about him and Julia. To silence them, he felt obliged to recall Domitia. The three proceeded to live happily in the palace, enlarging one more historical rumor to scandalous proportions.

Paris, the pantomime, imperial playboy, *bete noire* of the whole soap opera, was stabbed in the street by hired assassins, victim of a jealous rage (*saevitia*), which even today justifies some homicides. Dio Cassius' colorful second century account, with divorce, the street killing and the emperor's affair with Julia, to say nothing of the *menage a troix*, seems improbable.

As emperor, Domitian believed in Imperial power, with himself as monarch, surrounded by a court which would serve as his trusted council (*consilium*). His council accompanied him everywhere, whether to his Alban citadel (*arx Albina*) or on his many military campaigns. He went on five such campaigns, together with his retinue (*comitatus*), adding up to some three years' absence from Rome. An emperor's absence from Rome deprived the Senate of even a disguised sharing of power. Augustus would have warned the emperor against such behavior. He probably rarely attended Senate meetings, even while he was living on the Palatine, though there is no record of this, one way or the other. The influence of the Senate was further weakened because Domitian lived away from Rome more than any other emperor. He loved his villa at Alba on the Via Appia, about twenty kilometers from Rome. Here he enjoyed hunting--he was a skilled archer--and reading Tiberius's commentaries. Restful days and an evening breeze must have eased the stresses of being emperor.

Domitian put major emphasis on trusted friends (*amici*) for governing the Empire and serving as his counsellors. They were mostly senators but were also equestrians. They included generals, political leaders and the praetorian prefects. These *amici* formed the council. They were summoned when needed, and their selection was not based on family relatives or traditional leaders but on trust. This was the bottom line to qualify as one of the emperor's amici. Some resided at the Imperial palace for short periods. The Imperial residence included the emperor's family and a permanent administrative staff, the majority of whom were freedmen (*liberti*).

Domitian saw himself as the new Augustus. Money, morals and building were important to his reign. More than any other emperor, he wanted to be personally involved in the governing of Rome and the Empire. His first act was to revalue the currency by 12 per cent. He did this by putting back that amount of silver into the *denarius* (a coin). He ended the minting of bronze coins but resumed it again after two years. He had given the army a pay raise of one-third and had begun building roads and bridges across the Empire. Then, in 85, with Imperial revenue unable to meet spending costs, he had to devalue the denarius. Wars would drain the treasury, which had been well-stocked at Titus' death. Through rigid tax enforcement and by keeping the denarius stable, Domitian was able both to wage wars and build. It was the strict enforcement of tax collection that made this possible.

Rome was still not rebuilt after the fires of 64 and 80. Domitian had the temple of Jupiter on the Capitoline restored. He completed the Flavian Amphitheater by adding the fourth level and finishing the interior. Titus' temple to the deified Vespasian (*Divi Vespasiani*) was opened by January 87. (Three of its columns and the entablature rise above the mist on the southeastern slope of the Capitoline.) Several temples were rebuilt in Rome, and the *Forum Traianum* (Forum of Trajan) was begun. It is still standing, an awesome multistory mall with an open-air top-level walk, tying together stalls, halls and staircases.

Domitian was proud of the entirely new palace complex he had completed by the end of 92. Its four towering buildings covered 40,000 square meters, stretching across the summit of the Palatine Hill. Terraced and faced with marble, it remained the nerve center of the Roman Empire for centuries. (Today its bare brown bricks conjure up images of a time when deals were cut, legions were dispatched, scandals percolated and emperors were terminated.)

Domitian kept a very private devotion to Minerva. He enforced religious rites, as his model Augustus had done. He had three Vestal Virgins executed for incest (*incestum*). He also observed the traditional rites of the Saturnalia in December of each year, as well as every other state ceremony and tradition. He was highly respected in the East, where the people compared him to Nero. His *philhellenism* (respect for Greek culture) was remembered. A temple at Delphi was restored with his personal funds, and the temple of Artemis at Ephesus was enlarged. He promoted the building of roads and granted city status to many of the municipalities, which were more numerous in the East than in the West.

When Domitian appointed himself censor for life (*censor perpetuus*) in 85, he became responsible not only for admitting and removing senators and equestrians but also for the general morals of the people. He ended the practice of castration. He was strict in the punishment of corrupt officials. Administrative honesty rose noticeably in the provinces of the Empire during his reign.

Much has been written about the wholesale execution of Christians under Domitian. No evidence exists for this belief. (It arose only with some writings in the sixteenth century.) Nor were Jews persecuted. They had been suppressed in Judaea and driven out of their lands, but they were allowed to practice their religious observances. They were specifically obliged to pay an annual tax that supported the Capitolium in Rome. It had formerly gone to their own temple in Jerusalem, and they deeply resented this affront to their religion. It would eventually lead to a major revolt by the Jews.

In Spain many towns were raised to the status of municipality or colony. Latin rights were extended even further in the provinces, so that more and more people enjoyed a degree of self-government under Rome. Some provinces were reorganized. Germany was reduced to one military area. Public construction continued everywhere, but especially in the new province of Asia Minor.

While building reflected growth and prosperity under Rome's leadership, war took a major part of Domitian's time. Though not an expansionist, he was as aware as his predecessors of the importance of defense. During his reign the military focus shifted dramatically from Germany and Britain to the Balkans.

His first military contact was with the Chatti in northern Gaul. Going there in 82, ostensibly to take a census, he turned on the Chatti. He had waited twelve years for the glory of war and now seized the moment (*carpe diem!*). He waged war and installed roads, forts and watchtowers, beginning a system that would continue long after his time.

The Danube frontier was the next flashpoint of danger. The whole region was large and complex and merits a brief explanation. Rome had no fewer than eight Danubian provinces. Each had its northern border on the Danube river. This waterway had its headwaters in the Alps, as did the Rhine river. The Danube flows generally eastward with its mouth at the Black Sea.

This region was the backbone of the Roman Empire. Not only was it rich in villages, mining and agriculture, but it was also a prime recruiting ground for soldiers. Geographically, it was the bridge joining together the eastern and western sides of the Empire. The Danubian provinces were heavily armed, with six legionary camps and three fleets along the river banks. The camps located at *Castra Regina* (Regensburg), *Lauricum* (Lorch), *Vindobona* (Vienna), *Aquincum* (Budapest) and *Singidunum* (Belgrade) suggest the importance of the Danubian provinces.

When three Germanic tribes north of the Danube became restless and began amassing forces, Domitian ordered reinforcements from Germany. The Dacians, largest and most powerful of the tribes, then crossed the Danube, defeating the Romans. Domitian arrived in 85, invading Moesia, probably at Belgrade, and successfully drove the Dacians north of the Danube again.

When he returned to Rome, word reached him that Roman troops had invaded Dacia and had been soundly defeated. He returned to the Danube region again in August of 86 and divided Moesia into Upper and Lower (*Superior et Inferior*) provinces. He continued to build roads and ports and to create client-kingdoms.

Defense played a major role in Britain, as well. There Agricola, the brilliant consular legate, reported to Domitian in 81 that he foresaw victory over the entire island in another year. A new legionary fortress was built at Inchtuthill the following year, and Agricola spoke of taking Ireland next, with but one legion and auxiliaries. But because reinforcements were needed in Germany, Domitian drew vexillations (*vexillationes*, i.e., small units) from the four legions in Britain. With that, Agricola's dreams of glory were crushed.

More downsizing was to come. Between 87 and 88 fortresses in northern Scotland were abandoned by order of the emperor. The newly-built Inchtuthill, (located at 57 degrees NL) was completely taken apart. Clearly, Claudius would have disapproved. He had led the legions to the successful conquest of Britain in 43.

The devaluation of 85 brought on a flood of financial difficulties for the Empire, triggering a harsh reaction among Rome's numerous citizens. The strict collection of taxes in 86 brought several desert tribes of Africa to unite and defeat Roman forces in Numidia. They were soon brought under control. Still, like all rebellions, it required force. Like all empires, the Roman Empire offered two sides: both peace and war.

In January 89 Saturninus, the governor of Upper Germany at Mainz, declared against Domitian. Treason was the most ominous event for any emperor to deal with. The Chatti joined the two rebellious legions, but they were quickly suppressed by joint efforts. The commander of Lower Germany refused to rebel, and Trajan, summoned from Spain, and Domitian, marching with the Praetorian Guard, were able to control the situation. Reasons for this rebellion are uncertain. The opportunity for military advancement had shifted to the Balkan theater of operations, and certainly the scaling back of forces in Britain saw the hopes for military glory fade from both the British and German military commands. Still, the army had gained a salary increase from Domitian, and that sector of society would eventually mourn Domitian's death the most.

The Senate had many reasons to hate Domitian. He saw himself as a benevolent despot. When he had himself made censor for life, he was also elected consul for ten years in succession. Both these acts gave new meaning to the traditional imperium. Now he could create and remove senators freely, and he did so, prompted in part by his suspicious character. His father had rejected the delatores, who lived off petty accusations of treason. Domitian began to welcome them back, for he knew that his non-traditional appointments were bringing resentment. He had also spent about three years among the legions and was absent from Rome during 82-3, 85, 86 and 89, weakening the influence of the elites. According to Suetonius, the emperor was also motivated by greed. When condemnations were decreed, they led to confiscations of villas, and all other properties. Those could be sold to raise money for the state. Because Domitian was without heirs, the dynasty would end with him, and his name could be safely vilified. He would receive an official *damnatio memoriae*, the final payback to any emperor who had lost the support of the Senate and the people of Rome.

Like many emperors before him, Domitian wanted support from a new aristocracy, and he got this by bringing unfamiliar faces into the Senate and promoting them quickly, often disregarding the age and time limits for quaestor, aedile, praetor and senator. He shared consulships with non-Flavians, thus granting power and perquisites to rising families. Domitian thus disturbed many of the 600 senators who had served for years in hopes of a certain promotion to a position as governor of a province or legionary commander.

He had also concentrated power in the hands of a few trusted amici. They had formed his retinue while he was away from Rome, thus depriving the Senate of the chance to consult and approve his decisions. He, and not Trajan, first brought numbers of easterners into the power loop, which included the Senate, the equestrian class and his amici. (The new approach really began with Augustus.) Thus, while the Senate as a body became less powerful, those senators in the power loop would become more powerful. The proportion of non-Italians in the Senate under Domitian shifted from 33 to 38 per cent. As a proportion of non-Italians, Spain and Gaul dropped from 76 to 60 per cent. Easterners increased from 15 to 26 per cent.

The same shift was evident within the equestrian class. The emperor promoted many equestrians to trusted positions and created new administrative posts, filling them also with equestrians. Instead of relying on traditional patrician and senatorial families, he developed a power set that he felt he could trust. Clearly, he was his own man. Still, Domitian frequently offered positions of power to his opponents. He wanted to maintain the Senate. He had a concept of justice and decorum, but he wanted it on his very own terms.

Domitian was an enigma to many. Though he saw Augustus as his model, he was in many ways like Tiberius, whose commentaries he loved to read. Tiberius had not been Augustus's first choice for the succession, nor was Domitian. Both felt neglected by the emperor; both lacked a sense of humor and became introverted, spending time alone and in reading. Both offered the Empire a new agenda and found relief and release outside the Imperial city. Both were suspicious to the point where they could not mix with their peers. For Domitian it was a fatal flaw.

His anxieties about personal safety proved valid when, on 18 September of 96, he was stabbed to death. His wife Domitilla and the Praetorian Guard leaders were in on the plan, but the assassination came at the hands of some of his own amici. He was doomed by his suspicious nature, which led to executions, among both senators and his personal staff. He had alienated many senatorial families, most of whom were interrelated through marriage. He had weakened Rome's efforts in Britain. Still, he had brought Easterners into leadership positions and had extended power to new equestrians and senators. He had improved the administration of the Empire through close personal involvement. He had extended road-building and major constructions, many of which have survived to our time. The *damnatio memoriae* of the Senate followed quickly upon his death.

Part Two

The Second Century:

A Time of Maturing

The Five Good Emperors (AD 96-180)

V. Nerva and Trajan

Over the next eighty-two years five successful emperors would promote the *pax Romana* (Roman peace) throughout the Empire. Their peaceful succession from one to another came from the principle of adopting as "son and heir" the best man to be found in the Empire. This practice had been used before Nerva's time, but he made it a tradition. With the assassination of Domitian, who left no heirs, the Senate seized the momentum (*carpe momentum!*) and chose Nerva to be the next emperor.

At age 66, Nerva was the senatorial choice. He would grant the Senate the fresh air of freedom and yet not be obnoxious to the army. He was described as having a long neck, a thin face and an *aquiline* (hooked) nose. He was aging and colorless and would doubtless protect the Senate against retaliation for their individual roles in the tyrannicide. Nerva's father had been a close friend of Tiberius. The son had found favor with both Nero and Vespasian. He had shared the consulship with Vespasian in 71 and served again with Domitian in 90. Clearly, he had some prestige.

New coins recalling an emperor's image and accomplishments were the major way to spread information and propaganda throughout the Empire. By Nerva's orders, coins were now issued with the words *Libertas publica* (public freedom) and *Roma renascens* (Rome reborn). He also put an immediate stop to executions of senators.

The Praetorian Guard, though, were not pleased with Nerva as emperor. The Guard believed he had been involved in Domitian's death. They were aware that Domitian had removed and executed the two previous Guard commanders as part of his reign of terror. His new commanders, Petronius Secundus and Norbanus, had been in on the tyrannicide, for they knew very well that someone could have brought charges of *maiestas* (treason) against them at any time. Thus, it was with their complicity that Domitilla asked Stephanus to commit the act. It was Stephanus, palace servant and ex-slave, who stabbed Domitian while he was reading a report on a supposed conspiracy. In the violent combat with Domitian, the assassin was also killed.

The Guard now probably believed they could gain some influence over Nerva without having to start another civil war. Knowing how they felt, Nerva made a donative to the Guard as an act of clemency. This was reflected in one of the coins minted in his honor, carrying the words *Concordia Exercituum* (the harmony of the army).

Since Nerva's challenge was to make peace with all of society, he now embarked on repairing the capital. He built warehouses for grain, thus protecting the food supply and improving distribution. He repaired some aqueducts and granted land to the poor, selling some of his own property to pay for it. He also increased the exemptions from the inheritance tax. These acts were accompanied by his efforts to turn public opinion away from Domitian. Those whom he had exiled were allowed to return and reclaim their property. Nerva wanted to please all sides and heal the wounds.

Like Domitian before him, he listened to the *delatores*. It certainly helped him to learn of two possible plots on his life. There was even a mutiny on the Danube, though it didn't get very far. A more dangerous movement came from within the Praetorian Guard. The Guard demanded that Petronius Secundus be removed as commander. They held him responsible for the assassination. Nerva listened and, removing Secundus, appointed as the new prefect Caspinus (*Casperius*) Aelianus, one of Domitian's own amici. He now spoke for the Guard in demanding that Petronius Secundus, the former commander, and the freedman Parthenius, be handed over for execution. Rome was once again at the flashpoint! Some of the Guard broke into the palace in search of the two. Nerva stood in their way, offering his own life. Brushing him aside, they seized their quarry and, dragging them out, killed them. They even forced the jolted Nerva to thank the Guard.

With this incident behind him, Nerva had a new view of reality at the top. Sensing his loss of authority, he chose Trajan, the high-profile commander of the legions of Upper Germany, to co-rule as his "son and heir." Trajan was the most successful of the legionary commanders, and the decision met with the total approval of the military. This happened in October 97, and it removed a major threat to both Nerva and the peace which Rome so sorely wanted. Nerva died in January 98. The decision to select as heir the best man available--rather than a member of his own family--established a model for the next eighty years. The idea of hereditary leader did not die, but the next four emperors either had no children or they had died before their fathers.

Trajan

If Rome needed a prudent leader and a winning commander with a modest lifestyle, it found that unique combination in Marcius Ulpius Traianus. His family came originally from Tuder in Umbria, Italy, and settled at Italica in Spain's southern province of Baetica. There Trajan was born on 18 September in the year 52 (53?). His father had been a senator from Baetica, advancing through his merits to consul. Next, he was selected to be governor of Asia and Syria. His mother was most likely of Spanish origin, making Trajan the first non-Italian emperor.

He received an excellent elite education as a member of the aristocracy. Advancing through the *cursus honorum*, he spent ten years as a military tribune (*tribunus militum*) in Syria and was appointed to praetor in 85. He was next assigned to Spain as legionary commander and from there was summoned to help put down Saturninus's revolt in Upper Germany. Arriving after the uprising had ended, he was nevertheless recognized by Domitian as a trustworthy commander and was made legate (*legatus*) to Upper Germany, and then consul in 91. While serving as commander of forces in Upper Germany, he received Nerva's edict adopting him as "son and heir" and making him co-regent. The edict was dated 27 October 97. At

Nerva's death, Trajan remained for awhile in Upper Germany, then journeyed to the Danube region, strengthening fortifications and bringing the legions to combat-ready status.

Trajan was described as tall and well built. He had an aquiline nose on a big round face, and his straight-cut hair hung across a low forehead. As he and his escort arrived in Rome in 99, he conveyed the solemn air of *gravitas* (dignity), in keeping with the Roman tradition. He had traveled to Rome modestly, and upon entering the city gates, he walked behind his *lictors* (attendants of the magistrates), his wife Plotina at his side.

The procession wound its way among the temples and public buildings of the Forum, tracing the Via Sacra to the temple of Jupiter on the Capitoline. Beginning in 508 BC, all of Rome's major decisions and accomplishments were marked by a procession to the Capitolium, where prayer and sacrifice linked with tradition to confirm the bond between past and present. Entering the temple, Trajan gazed at the statues of its three deities. Standing on the spot where Nerva had adopted him, he offered prayers and a bovine sacrifice for a successful reign. There he would also deify his godfather Nerva.

His Administrative Changes

Trajan's years would be marked by numerous administrative and military changes. Even before reaching Rome, he had ordered the Praetorian commander, Caspinus Aelianus, executed. Wanting to appear tolerant and respectful of all, he would ask the Senate's approval of legislation and treaties. Striving for partnership between Senate and princeps, he directed that the delatores be exiled. He wanted to end the conspiratorial atmosphere that had so often existed in the Curia, so he discouraged trials for treason.

If he returned an atmosphere of freedom to the Senate, he still believed certain precautions were necessary. He developed a secret service, using the couriers (*frumentarii*), who reported on the crucial grain supply, as double agents. He also formed a new bodyguard. Comprised of select cavalry (*equites singulares*) from Germany and

Pannonia, it numbered a thousand strong and served the emperor faithfully in all his expeditions.

Among his major reforms was the removal of the five per cent tax on the inheritance of persons who were not born citizens. This inheritance tax had seemed very unfair to all who had to pay it. The same tax was ended for those earning below a certain wage. He was also able to reduce the customary donative to the soldiers by half, without any mutinies following. Attending to the needs of the people, Trajan continued the free grain dole, even with more mouths to feed. He established a system of financial subsidies (*alimenta*) for poor children.

Trajan's success with the tax system was remarkable but was made possible because of his administrative economy and the spoils of his Dacian wars. As was noted, he sent commissioners (agents) into the towns of Italy, as well as the free cities of the Imperial and senatorial provinces. These agents checked on the magistrates and improved the tax collections. Under Nerva several governors were accused of accepting graft. These were removed and prosecuted by special administrators (*curator reipublicae*); for whole provinces, they were called *corrector reipublicae*, who were assigned to correct provincial and local finances when that became necessary. They extended the influence of the emperor everywhere, centralizing control and weakening senatorial influence in the cities. Through their work in the free cities they reduced the privileges of the Empire. The Imperial intervention tended to equalize all the cities of the Empire. Trajan was also careful in appointing provincial governors.

The best example of these curators was Pliny the Younger, a senator assigned by Trajan to Bithynia. Pliny wrote a number of letters back to Trajan in the form of reports. In them he describes conditions, points out problems, outlining his plans, and seeking advice and decisions from the emperor. The letters reflect Trajan's genuine interest in the welfare of the provinces. His humane treatment of the people reflected a broad, empire-wide view that was fast replacing the once-provincial approach from Rome.

Trajan in fact seemed preoccupied with interfering in the affairs of the self-governing cities. Yet, it was necessary for the special curators to step in because of one very disturbing change that occurred during the first and second centuries. The general public (*plebs*) had the authority to elect magistrates in their cities. The magistrates formed the city senate and were counted among the urban elites. They held very competitive positions, and overall, they were dedicated to serving the citizens of their municipalities. They often donated their own money for needs such as aqueducts, roads and schools.

In the struggle for power, the right to choose their leaders was gradually taken from the plebs by the magistrates. Customs slowly transformed into rules which required a newly elected magistrate to contribute to the city treasury or to launch some major public work. In time, the less wealthy families were forced to drop out of running for office, as they could not afford the large required donations.

Some magistrates offered elaborate entertainments, like gladiatorial combats, instead of financing needed repairs to roads and bridges. The slow shift in attitude and custom left fewer men to rule their cities, but they were among the wealthiest. And, as spectacular gifts were expected by magistrates, the plebs began to view the contributions by the few as a substitute for taxes. The collection and payment of local taxes soon slipped into default. Government in the hands of the few was not working, and towns soon became indebted. Imperial curators were Trajan's solution to deal with these fiscal problems of the cities. Imperial intervention tended to equalize all the cities of the Empire, and Italy received no special treatment thereafter.

If the tax system helped shift power toward the Imperial palace, and away from the Curia, Trajan hurried that process in still another way: he appointed many new members to the equestrian class, doing this without holding the title of censor. By disregarding the power of the censor, he helped reshape the authority of the emperor, raising it to new heights of absolutism.

Under Trajan the state allowed low-interest loans to small landowners, encouraging both land ownership and, especially, more grain production. To improve upon Nerva's system of *alimenta*, the interest from these loans was handed over to the urban magistrates for the support of needy children. By paying a subsidy to needy parents and orphans, Trajan hoped to promote the growth of families. His administration was so ready to be open and honest with the people that it published a budget, showing government expenses.

To stop emigration from Italy, the emperor issued an ordinance that no Italians should be sent to start new colonies. This reflected his thinking that the provinces should help the mother-country. It was inconsistent because the Roman legions were getting most of their recruits from the provinces, so the provincial contribution was already significant.

Concerned also with communication in an ever-growing Empire, the emperor reorganized the postal system (*cursus publicus*). At its head he appointed an equestrian with the new title, *praefectus vehiculorum* (transportation supervisor). It was his task to have horses and carriages prepared for use in the postal service throughout Italy. The next emperor would further develop this service.

His Building Legacy

Virtually every emperor left temples, baths, roads or a forum as monuments to his reign and memory. Trajan's public works program was awesome. He advanced the network of roads and bridges, especially in Dacia, Syria and the Transjordan. He improved communication from Rome to Brundisium by a new road across the Apennines. He commissioned the last aqueduct for Rome. Known as the *Aqua Traiana*, it had its source in the springs near Lake Sabatinus. It ran from there to the Janiculum Hill, servicing that area before crossing the Tiber River and ending on the Esquiline Hill.

Trajan's Baths, also on the Esquiline, were built on a wing of Nero's Golden House. Designed by Trajan's architect, Apollodorus of Damascus, the new attraction opened in 109 and was the first of the truly large baths built in Rome.

Trajan's Forum (*Forum Traianum*) was the largest and most splendid of the *fora* (forums) of Rome. Designed by Apollodorus, it was formed by cutting away part of the Quirinal Hill. It measured 182x120 yards. (Its magnificent ruins can still be admired.) The Column of Trajan, erected in the center by the Senate to

commemorate his Dacian wars, soared 100 feet into the air. Low
reliefs spiral around it, recounting the story of his conquests. It was
flanked by Greek and Latin libraries (*Bibliotheca Ulpia*), which are
no longer standing. A harbor was built at Ancona during Trajan's
reign to relieve the busy port of Ostia. That port, located at the
mouth of the Tiber, was redesigned with both inner and outer harbors.

His Foreign Affairs

At the beginning of Trajan's reign, the Empire's natural border
extended roughly along the Rhine-Danube frontier (*limes*) in the north,
to the Euphrates in the east. The major threat to the frontier had been
the Dacian tribes just north of the Danube. These tribes were
becoming more mobile as they grew in numbers. It is not clear
whether they were being pushed southward by more northerly tribes
or whether they were making allies to cross into the Roman provinces.
It was Trajan's first objective simply to prevent the consolidation of
those barbarians into a rival and threat.

After offering sacrifices at Rome on 25 March of 101, Trajan
launched his first Dacian campaign. One legion was brought from
Lower Germany to join eight already in the provinces of the Danube
region. Total troop strength numbered about 60,000 men.

Trajan directed the assault upon Dacia himself, but he was assisted by
able commanders. One of these was Hadrian. Married to Trajan's
grand-niece Julia Sabina, he took his place among the Imperial retinue
(*comites*). As the oldest male relative of the emperor, he would some
day be named "son and heir."

Establishing fortresses in Dacian territory, Trajan returned to nearby
Pannonia to winter. In the spring of 102 he set out by boat to
Viminacium (Kostolac) to gather his forces. Crossing the Danube, the
legionaries headed for the Dacian capital of Sarmizegetusa. Trajan
split his legions to effect a pincer movement. It was a brilliant
strategy. When battle was engaged, the Dacians resisted fiercely.
Rome's German and Mauretanian cavalry were matched by deadly
Sarmatian mounted archers. Legion clashed with deadly tribal
formation.

Still, it was not enough. Driving through rugged forest-covered mountain passes, the legions came at last to the capital. King Decebalus surrendered, and Dacia was forced to accept terms, making it a dependency of Rome. Its weapons were destroyed, its deserters and prisoners were exchanged, its fortresses were occupied by legionary detachments, and some territory was ceded. The Dacians were bound never to declare war or make peace without Rome's consent.

With this, Trajan's forces withdrew to Rome. With the plunder, Trajan offered the masses a great *congiarium* (dole). With the submission of Decebalus, the emperor had hoped to end forever the Germanic threat to the Danube; however, very soon the Dacians began to rearm. Overrunning the Roman fortresses in their territory, they made it very clear that the treaty was history.

At this turn of events, Trajan and his council decided to depart from the recognized Augustan policy of not expanding the Empire's borders. Dacia would be made a Roman province. Orders were now dispatched to the legionary commanders of both German provinces to proceed with all four legions. The emperor's council, together with the Imperial cavalry, after lengthy preparations, moved out of Rome en masse in 104 and again headed northward to the Danube.

Trajan's plan called for bypassing the earlier staging ground of Viminacium in favor of Egeta, about five days farther down-river. On his orders, a massive stone bridge was built at Drobeta (*Turnu Severin*). Designed by Apollodorus, it had 20 stone piers, each 150 feet high and 60 feet wide. They were spaced at 120-foot intervals and joined by arches, probably constructed of wood. (Some historians believe this was the greatest architectural accomplishment of Trajan's time. The piers are still visible.)

A battle-hardened army formed a spirited procession as it tongued its way across the Danube by boat and bridge: 11,000 irregular forces, representing dozens of ethnicities and drawn up into units of 300 men (*numeri*); just behind them came more than 200,000 auxiliary forces, forming a babel of tongues. On their heels marched the bulk of Rome's army, perhaps 60,000 legionaries, the majority of them of provincial origins. Trajan had always wanted to emulate Julius

Caesar. The way was now open to etch his name forever in the annals of Rome's conquests.

In the operations that followed (AD 105-06), the Romans met their match in the tactics and firepower of warfare. Many of the tribesmen of Dacia had been trained by the legions, and they were well-equipped in both arms and armor. Still, Rome's destiny was not to be denied. The capital was captured and destroyed, the survivors scattered. Many of Decebalus's nobles met for a last banquet and drank a cup of poison. The king himself was pursued until he was surrounded and chose to cut his throat. He was decapitated and his head brought to the Roman camp. It was then sent by Trajan to Rome, there to be displayed in the Forum.

This was the last major conquest of Rome to stand the test of time. Some 50,000 survivors among the Dacian tribes were enslaved and marched to Rome, to meet their fate in a more horrible fashion in the Colosseum. Their land was repopulated with settlers drawn especially from Syria and Asia Minor. A new capital was raised near the old one and was named Ulpia Traiana. Three German legions remained on the Danube, and Pannonia was split into Upper and Lower provinces. Much gold, silver and other booty was taken from Dacia and brought to Rome.

When Trajan returned late in 107, he was met with shouts of *"Optimus"* ("the best"). He offered celebrations lasting 126 days, featuring 10,000 gladiators and savage wild-animal hunts. The masses received a congiarium, their third of Trajan's reign. The first, in the year 99, had amounted to 75 denarii, the same as Nerva had given. After each of the Dacian wars, it rose to 650 denarii a head, a reflection of the plunder of the campaigns. The emperor also extended the *pomerium* (boundary marker) of Rome as part of the celebrations.

The Senate voted to erect the Column of Trajan. Its somberly realistic scenes are sculpted in a band spiraling around a 100-foot column. They form the only record of events. Trajan's own commentaries have been lost to history.

The cost of the victory celebrations, as well as the wars themselves and the ending of some taxes during Trajan's reign, were made possible by the plunder of the Dacian campaigns. Valuable mines in the north had produced much gold, and slaves and other plunder were sold for revenue. No precise records exist for the agricultural production of the new province of Dacia (part of Romania), but it was enormous and produced lasting benefit to the Empire.

Filled with confidence from his successes in central Europe, Trajan now turned his attention to the East. There Chosroes, the king of Parthia, had offended Rome's dignity by crowning his nephew Exedares (Axidares) as king of Armenia. Client-kings were expected to journey to Rome to be crowned, but Chosroes was in fact treating Armenia as his own vassal state.

Brushing diplomacy aside, Trajan led forces into Syria, deposed the Armenian pretender, and annexed Armenia (eastern Turkey). It became for the first time a Roman province, though this would not last long. With this victory Trajan added the name *Optimus* (the best) to his growing list of titles. From Armenia he invaded Mesopotamia, accepting the submission of Arab kings and building roads as he and the legions breached the desert sands. After organizing Mesopotamia as a province, he fell back and wintered at Antioch in 115-16. Before doing so, he ordered a fleet constructed on the Euphrates River, the eastward boundary of the Empire since the time of Augustus.

Early the next spring Trajan's forces attacked the upper Tigris River region of Adiabene. It was overrun and annexed as the province of Assyria. Rejoining his fleet on the Euphrates, the emperor directed his legions to make a parallel march along the two rivers. Ancient Babylon, nearly deserted, fell an easy prey, but the objective was to take Ctesiphon, Chosroes' capital on the Tigris (about ten miles south of modern Baghdad).

With the siege of the capital, Chosroes fled, though his daughter was captured, together with the golden throne of the Parthian kings. *Parthia capta* (Parthia captured) was inscribed on coins marking the event.

Naming Chosroes' son as king, the princeps proceeded to sail down the Tigris to its mouth in 116. There he viewed the vast Persian Gulf, the first western emperor since Alexander the Great to reach its warm waters. Seeing vessels embarking for India, he recalled Alexander and wished that he, too, could continue on to India. Trajan had extended the Roman Empire to its greatest limits, covering an area of 1.7 million square miles. In so doing, he had projected Roman power beyond the limits set by Augustus.

Retracing their steps across the vast desert, the Roman legions learned with misgivings that their earlier conquests were coming undone. Their lightning strikes had overrun Mesopotamia and the Arab lands but had not conquered them. The Parthians were in revolt, and Chosroes himself was suspected of fomenting a widespread rebellion among the Jewish communities of the eastern provinces. Judaea itself, where Roman forts had been weakened in order to engage the Parthians, was an armed camp.

The uprisings were serious, spreading through very large Jewish communities. First in Cyrenaica in 115, then spreading across to Cyprus, Egypt, Palestine and Mesopotamia, the Jews of the *Diaspora* (Dispersion) had reached the flashpoint of civil disobedience during Trajan's eastern campaign. The motives for these stirrings included the Messianic hopes of the Jews. Their disgust with the punitive tax on their communities (*fiscus Iudaicus*) and the loss of trade with devastated Parthian towns were also factors.

The first objective of their uprisings were the Hellenic communities of the Levant. With their many gods and earthly views, the Greeks had always been a contradiction to the biblical ideals of the Jews. Indiscriminate slaughter of civilians now took place everywhere Jewish and Greek communities were found together. When Roman legions were finally dispatched to the cities, military action was swift and severe.

Once the rebellions were under control, Trajan felt obliged to prepare for another campaign into Mesopotamia. While at Antioch, his temporary quarters, he took ill and left for Rome. Reaching Selinus, a city in Cilicia, he could go no farther. His grave condition, described as dropsy, was followed by a stroke. On his deathbed, the emperor finally adopted as son and heir his closest male relative and most trusted officer, Publius Aelius Hadrianus, husband of his grand-niece. Trajan died at Selinus, on 8 August of 117, in the presence of his wife Plotina. His ashes were carried to Rome, where they were laid to rest in a vault at the base of the Column of Trajan. The imposing shrine forms a record of one of Rome's greatest emperors. A symbol of the last province to bend to the sway of Roman power, the Column seems destined to stand as long as Rome itself.

VI. Hadrian

To Hadrian fell the task of continuing the administrative and fiscal, social and military reforms of the Empire. Yet, Hadrian approached all these with such breadth of vision, and such a sense of organization and finality that he stands out as the most illustrious and creative of all the emperors to his time, perhaps of all time. Moreover, his architectural designs and his foreign affairs decisions left a legacy that bound together the East and West in ways unimagined before his time. During his reign the Rome of pagan polytheism turned eastward in search of mystical religious experiences. In that quest it gained a new understanding of the differences between polytheism and monotheism. Also during his time, like a butterfly rising from its cocoon, Christianity would begin to soar away from Jewry on wings of its own.

Hadrian was born at Rome (Syme: 10 f; at Italica, Lambert: 31 f) on January 26th in the year 76. His family, the Aelii, hailed from the town of Italica, near *Hispalis* (Seville), in the Roman province of *Baetica* (Spain). His ancestors had emigrated from Hadria, a small Italian town along the Adriatic (*Hadriatic*) Sea. They were among the founders of this Italian colony (hence Italica), begun by Sc. Africanus after the Carthaginians had been defeated in Spain in 205 BC. Since his mother was from Gades (Cadiz), Hadrian was, like his relative Trajan, a provincial of mixed parentage.

Hadrian was a fair-skinned man of taller than average height. Well-built and with blue-grey eyes, he must have caught the attention of

85

those in his presence. His hair was combed down over brows covered by curls fashioned by hot tongs. He wore a short beard, restarting a trend that had gone out of fashion during the Republic.

Hadrian's father died when the boy was just ten, and Trajan, his nearest male relative, took him to Rome as his guardian. It was while he was at Rome that Hadrian fell in love with Greek culture and language. He returned to Italica after five years, there to revel in the open spaces, the rich and forested land on the Baetic River, which shaped his love for hunting. He also learned to play the flute and developed a flair for poetry. This rich and diverse background reflected the ideals of the philhellene he was.

At age seventeen he was taken by his brother-in-law Servianus to Rome, there to enter the cursus honorum. After appointments to several minor magistracies, the first in Probate court, he was sent to *Aquincum* (Budapest) as *tribune* (military officer). From there he was assigned to Lower *Moesia* (eastern Bulgaria). Hadrian was in Germany when Trajan was named co-regent. The 21-year-old youth would accompany his guardian back to Rome in 99.

Early in his career, Hadrian married Vibia Sabina, about whom little is known. It was not a happy marriage, yet the two stayed together as a matter of decorum.

By 101 he was made quaestor, serving on the Imperial staff with responsibilities such as reading messages to the Senate. In 105 he was nominated tribune of the people. The position had lost its function since Republican days but carried prestige as a representative of the plebs. He accompanied Trajan on his second Dacian campaign. There he commanded a legion so successfully that Trajan gave him a diamond ring that had been presented to him by Nerva. It was a nonverbal communication that carried a major message. Hadrian now had one more reason to believe he would be "son and heir."

Within a year he was *praetor* (judge) and in 107 became governor of Lower Pannonia (eastern Hungary). Appointed consul (suffect) at age 33, he would serve as a close confidant of the emperor and write all his speeches. Though the position seemed to be grooming Hadrian to succeed his cousin someday, this relationship was never openly acknowledged. If Hadrian was the crown prince, he was certainly not the co-regent. Adoption came only on Trajan's deathbed. A rumor even arose at that time that Trajan's wife Plotina had signed the adopting papers herself--after the emperor's death. Whether or not there is evidence for this, Hadrian and Plotina got along very well, and she helped advance his career, no doubt by offering strong moral support.

Hadrian would accompany the princeps in all his campaigns, right down to the Jewish revolt. Trajan entrusted Hadrian with the governorship of Syria just before the eastern campaign. This was the cornerstone province of the *Levant* (eastern Mediterranean) and thus cast Hadrian in a major role in the East.

If, as history has recorded, Trajan granted no special favors to Hadrian, the son of his cousin, it simply adds to the enigma of Hadrian and their relationship. One author claims that the two shared a trait common at that time, viz., a love for boys and young men (Lambert: 33). Could that relationship (pederasty) have existed while Hadrian was in the care of his guardian? There never appeared any hostility between the two while Trajan was emperor, nor was there disagreement over state policy. Pederasty had long been practiced in Greece and only came to the attention of Rome after the conquest of that province (146 BC). It gained slow acceptance in the West until, by the second century, bisexuality had become a prominent fixture of upper class mores. Viewed with but a small stigma, it simply reflected the fashions of a sensuous and amoral society.

Unity

For Hadrian, life as emperor meant innovating, finding new means to fit old goals and improving social conditions. In sympathy with the needs of the provinces, he spent over half his reign visiting and inspecting thirty-eight of the forty-four provinces. Of those he did not personally review, he required written reports of their governors. He believed that his tours were necessary for the effective administration of the Empire. He loved to tour the land, review the legions, order improvements and leave buildings under construction. This was his lofty goal, to bind the Empire together.

Hadrian believed also in equality of treatment for the provinces. Italy, which had already seen a growing number of non-Italian senators and Imperial officials, would no longer receive special treatment. In promoting this cosmopolitan view, as opposed to a narrow, provincial outlook, Hadrian was more than just a product of the times and the trends. He orchestrated the thesis of dual cultures within a unified Empire. He not only represented his times; he led the very currents of which he was so important a part. His beard came in imitation of the Greek philosophers he loved and admired.

Peace and prosperity were blanketed across the Mediterranean land. Trade goods reached from Britain to the Euphrates. The roads had become a safe and reliable means of travel. And through his Imperial council, the princeps was demonstrating his belief that "the ruler exists for the state and not the state for the ruler" (Boak & Sinnigen: 330). The provinces should be tied to the emperor by love and not by fear. In effect, one could see in all five good emperors the principle of humanity, radiating from the Palatine. It appeared first in domestic changes, which would touch every province, from milestone to milestone. It must have been at this very time that the name Rome, "the capital city," gave way to the broader name "Roman," so that anyone, whether living in London, Lyon, Mainz, Belgrade, Athens or a Nile village, could claim proudly, "*Romanus sum*" (I am a Roman).

Foreign Affairs

Foreign affairs were to capture the new emperor's restive energy at once. He adopted a broad defensive approach as the cornerstone to foreign policy. He would strengthen the boundaries (*limites*, hence limits) of the frontier to make possible a prosperous state within. Trajan's Parthian wars had depleted the treasury, yet they had not brought peace in the East: Armenia and Mesopotamia were still in rebellion, and troubles were already reported in Mauretania, Britain and on the lower Danube. The Jewish rebellion had just been suppressed.

With the death of Trajan, Hadrian was acknowledged as emperor; at the time he was at Antioch, commanding five legions. All threw him their support unanimously. To have considered renewing warfare with

Parthia now would have cost new taxes from a weak treasury, and many other frontiers begged his urgent attention.

Hadrian's first act was to recognize Chosroes as king of Parthia, settling the question of Mesopotamia once and for all. He then withdrew forces from Armenia, granting the region autonomy. Thus, Hadrian's defensive policy had its first application here. The Syrian desert was far too large ever to conduct military operations there. To Hadrian it was (and is still) a natural frontier which had given birth to a cultural frontier where Roman influence never left an imprint. The Euphrates border established by Augustus had withstood the test of time.

Dispatching Turbo, his leading commander, to suppress the Jewish uprising, Hadrian marched quickly to Rome, arriving the 9th of July in 118. He wanted to make peace quickly with the Senate. While he was in the East the Praetorian Prefect Attianus, in Rome, had ordered the deaths of four ex-senators of consular rank, two of them leading generals, on charges of treason. Clearly upset with such a harsh measure, Hadrian still wanted to deal carefully with Attianus. He convinced him to resign and then appointed him senator.

The emperor took the same oath as his predecessors, never to condemn a senator without a trial by his peers. He made friends with the senatorial power loop, to the extent he could, and he always stood at the approach of a senator. Frequently senators were invited to dine with him, and he asked them to join him if he saw them while riding in his carriage. He was helpful to those senators who had slipped into poverty. He liked to visit them at their villas, and he was thoughtful in journeying to their homes when they were ill.

Administrative Reforms

Of all of Hadrian's reforms, the greatest were in the field of law. He made improvements to the legal system of the Empire that would endure for centuries. First, to speed up civil cases in the praetor's courts at Rome, he divided Italy into four districts, outside of Rome, assigning a judge of consular rank (*iuridicus consularis*) to each district. They relieved the praetor's courts at Rome of their crowded case loads. They tried cases of guardianship, wills with third parties (*fidei commissa*) and other trusts. They probably also heard appeals from the municipal courts.

This ordinance moved Imperial control beyond Trajan's reforms, though his fiscal agents (*curatores reipublicae*) continued their work in each province. It also removed the Senate from another sector of influence, effectively widening the gap between the senators--the former representatives of the people--and the burgeoning authority of the emperor. Through his Imperial bureaucracy he would make inevitable the rise of kings on the future chessboard of a shattered empire. If the trend of the times was to level the differences between Rome, Italy and the other provinces, it was also to sharpen the differences between emperor and elites.

Hadrian appointed more distinguished jurists to his legal advisory (*consilium principis*), making it a permanent standing body. Members (*consiliarii Augusti*) were almost entirely selected from among senators and equestrians, but Senate approval was required.

These jurists (*prudentes*) were granted the right to give a legal opinion (*ius respondendi*) on questions submitted to them. When their opinion (*responsa*) was unanimous, it carried the force of law, binding those judges trying similar cases. If their opinions differed, the judge could reach his own decision.

Up to Hadrian's time, new Roman laws and probably also the edicts of the provincial governors, were publicized annually by the new praetors. Known as the Perpetual Edicts of the praetor, or the "Praetor's Edict," they stated the laws and methods each praetor would follow that year. The collection had grown into a large and tangled body of laws and rules, many contradictory. Hadrian assigned his leading jurist, Salvius Julianus, to edit these principles and procedures of the law. In 131 his edition of the Edict was confirmed by the Senate as the embodiment of Roman law. Thereafter the Edict (*edictum perpetuum*) could be changed only by the emperor or the Senate. In effect, the supreme law of the Empire would now have its source in the emperors alone. Their statutes (*constitutiones principum*) became the sources of law. By the early second century, also, the ancient Comitia, the assembly that had formulated laws on behalf of the people (*leges populi*), had become a mere footnote of Republican memory. Now the emperor, with the advice of his council, stood unchallenged as the lawgiver.

Hadrian, with his "mastery of administrative routine" (Cary: 633), was a capable systems analyst, adept in the financial matters of the Empire. When he found the treasury in tax arrears by 900 million sesterces, he simply forgave all these debts in one stroke of the pen, hoping to spread goodwill. It began a practice that emperors would follow every fifteen years.

An equestrian was appointed the new finance minister, and the finance department was absorbed into the civil service. The system of farming out tax collection in the provinces to private companies was all but ended under Trajan and Hadrian. They appointed Imperial procurators to take over this task, adding to the centralizing trend. A standing committee, the *decemviri*, selected from senators and community leaders, seems to have had a major responsibility in this matter (Cary: 638).

Hadrian allowed tax exemptions for importers of essential foods into Rome. Towns struck by natural disasters were also granted tax exemptions. With these policies in place, Hadrian's administration was still able to balance the budget annually. It reflected a sound policy, bent on keeping peace within, and barbarians outside, the limits of the Empire.

Hadrian adopted a humane approach to human relationships. He revived an old law forbidding masters to kill their slaves. Instead, they were now required to hand them over to the law. He forbade their sale for immoral reasons or for use in the arenas, and he punished the ill-treatment of slaves. He could not alter the practice of torturing slaves to get their true testimony, but on another issue he was successful: instead of condemning all his slaves when a master was slain, now only those near enough to have helped prevent the crime were condemned.

His interests touched even the little details of civil life. He ordered stricter controls at the public baths, restricting their usage to women alone in the mornings. Senators and knights were required to wear the toga in public. The exception was their returning from dinner in the evening. He restricted large wagons from passing through Rome's narrow streets by day.

His social tinkering was also directed at the elite classes. He enhanced the equestrians' status by appointing them rather than freedmen to the secretariats. He established a two-track career path-- one military and one civilian. This meant that the young men had to choose their interests: civil or military. It forced them to specialize and develop their skills. It professionalized both tracks much more, transforming them into competitive programs. The princeps also created a team of attorneys (*advocati fisci*) to prosecute cases on behalf of the state treasury. Because of the increased flow of reports from the East, he appointed one secretary for Latin and another for Greek reports.

Though all five good emperors successfully improved their relations with the Senate, that body distrusted Hadrian because of the executions at the beginning of his reign. Relations only got worse over time. Despite their deference to the Senate, the same five emperors wanted to increase the power of the Flavians. All continued the policy of assigning the higher posts to equestrians if they were not already reserved for senators. Freedmen in the Imperial household were no longer assigned civil service posts.

Touring and Building the Provinces

In between his reforms at Rome, Hadrian took two major tours of the Empire. The first of these lasted five years, from 121 to 125. After offering sacrifice to begin his cult worship of Venus and Roma, on April 21st, 121, he embarked for the Rhine-Danube frontier, the *Agri Decumates*. The gap between the two rivers' headwaters was considered a major weakness. Bold tribes could force their way through the snow-clad mountain passes and invade Italy itself. The policy of strengthening this area was begun by Vespasian and continued by Domitian and Trajan. Hadrian began a series of walls to improve the forts already in place. He also increased the number of forts, locating them in better defensive positions. In so doing, he extended the defensive chain eastward of the Rhine and northward of the Danube in that area.

In the princeps' view, the Empire must reflect unity: unity of all people, all pulling for peace and prosperity. He respected the hundreds of languages and gods encompassed within the Empire but wanted the citizens to respect a common heritage, embodied in the Greco-Roman culture. He didn't enforce unity through conformity. Rather, he wanted each culture and each region to contribute to the whole as it developed.

The Empire was so large, and Hadrian recognized that better than anyone else through his tours. His love for travel and need to see things firsthand, together with his desire for building, brought into being many new roads, aqueducts, temples, colosseums and baths across the Mediterranean landscape. Some sixty million people in forty-four provinces would bond or separate, depending on the benefits of Roman citizenship and some focus to rally around.

Hadrian saw himself as the bridge between Athens and Zeus, on the one side, and Rome and Jupiter on the other. He wanted to be the force that brought unity through a common culture within a familiar set of languages and gods. To speed up this process, he wanted to combine the civil with the military life on the frontier. This would encourage the growth of towns, the nucleus of culture. Local merchants and craftsmen naturally gathered near frontier outposts. These people lived in settlements (*canabae*, i.e., booths) outside the camps. Veterans, too, when discharged, stayed nearby with their families. Hadrian started such colonies at two legionary headquarters on the Danube, Aquincum (Budapest) and Mursa (Osijek). He also converted into cities the legionary camps at Vindobona (Vienna), Carnuntum (Petronell), Viminacium (Kostolac) and Augusta Vindelicorum (Augsburg).

Continuing his tour of the provinces, he passed through Batavia (Holland) and then into Britain the next year. There he directed a battery of engineers, architects and craftsmen to construct the great defensive works known as Hadrian's Wall, in northern Britain. Really a system of walls, earthworks, *fosses* (ditches) and forts, it was flanked by a parallel road to the south. The walls were meant to last. They were about six to eight feet thick and twenty feet high. They enclosed lookout towers and fortified gates. Cavalry and infantry could charge northward or southward. The Wall extended from Segedunum (Walls-end) in the east to Maia (Bowness) on the Solway Firth (bay) in the west, a distance of seventy miles. From here the Roman legions would have a safe haven from which to sally forth at the first sign of tribal aggression. The legions had just fought a rebellion that lasted two years (119-21). Peace through strength would be achieved through strong defense and a fully prepared military.

Leaving Britain, he visited Spain, endowing his hometown and other cities with new buildings. Then crossing the Mediterranean, he toured Mauretania, Africa, and Asia, always inspecting, marching with the legions and sharing their food and camps. He helped decide on new forts and reveled in the beauty of desert, mountains and seacoast. Listening to the magistrates, he authorized aqueducts, basilicas, and temples. An inscription at Lambaesis (Lambese) in Numidia (Tunisia) records a speech by Hadrian to the troops. As he stood bareheaded in the boiling sun of that remote desert outpost, he called upon them to be ready to live up to Roman ideals.

Hadrian was the first emperor to visit Carthage since Scipio Africanus. Renaming the city Hadrianopolis, he stood on its wharves as ships, laden with caged animals, weighed anchor and set sail for Rome and the Colosseum. Continuing his city-building program, he made both Utica (Utique) and Zama new colonies before sailing off.

Inspecting, criticizing, improving and rewarding, he set forth policies that would remain in force for hundreds of years. Because he stressed local recruiting, he was responsible more than any other emperor for the new direction: the "Roman" army was now a "provincial" army. The legions now had a personal interest in protecting their borders. But for how long could they keep themselves within the borders and their relatives outside? Meantime, the Praetorian Guard would remain the only all-Italian unit; its elite officers would be sent out to the provinces as instructors.

Passing through Asia (Turkey), he visited Claudiopolis (Bithynios) in June of 123, ordering restorations and new buildings. It was here, in

Antinous's hometown, that he might first have met the boy of eleven or twelve that would play such a major role in his private life (Lambert: 59ff). Antinous would become his constant companion, nurture his sense of affection and drive his philhellenic instincts until one fateful day along the Nile.

During his stay in Greece, Hadrian was initiated into the Eleusinian mystery cult and began major buildings everywhere he went. In Athens he started a new city, the "City of Hadrian," at the foot of the Acropolis. In a spirit of magnanimity he commissioned an aqueduct, a temple and other structures in the city that captivated him. Everywhere he participated in temple worship and held his own in discussions with leading Greek thinkers.

By September of 125 the emperor was back at Rome. The next spring his boundless energy would be spent in beginning construction of his villa at Tibur (Tivoli), fifteen miles from the capital. Its lavish buildings would imitate the great edifices that inspired him in his distant travels. They would reflect both his eclectic tastes and his architectural flamboyance. Covering 750 acres, the villa was three-quarters the size of Rome. Its unifying feature was water. Controlled by a hydraulic system, Tivoli contained canals, reflecting pools and a moated pavilion, the *Nymphaeum*. The baths and palace were marvels that kept alive Hadrian's love for travel. One of the most copied structures is the *Canopus*, a large rectangular pool, surrounded by life-size statues of gods and heroes, all framed by columns that support architraves and arches. The emperor had seen such a pool at Canopus in Egypt.

Brick and concrete describe a stadium, a praetorium, the *Lyceum*, the *Serapeum*, guest rooms and a subterranean corridor, reminder of Hades itself. Traces of stucco and exquisite floors of black and white mosaics (*tesserae*) reveal a mind rich in thought, complex in taste and tolerant of mankind.

On April 21st of 128, the anniversary date of Rome's founding (April 21, 753 BC), Hadrian laid the foundation of a temple, dedicating it to Venus and Roma (*Templum Veneris et Romae*). Just seven years earlier, on April 21st, he had started a cult at Rome, entrusting the city and Empire to these two unifying symbols to rally the people.

Designed by Hadrian, the temple would be Rome's largest and would serve as the focal point of religion for ages to come. To make room for such a temple, the 99-foot statue of Nero (*Colossus*) had to be removed from its place in front of the Colosseum. (It was pulled in a standing position by 24 elephants.)

The famed Apollodorus advised the emperor that the new temple should set on a podium. Criticizing the size of the statues that were to go inside, he noted: "If the goddesses wanted to get up and go out, they'd hit their heads on the ceiling" (Perowne: 109). Hadrian was not pleased with the comment. He had always been one to reject and make fun of the experts. Still, he built the temple on a podium, adding a touch of majesty with two ten-columned porticoes. (Fifteen of the massive columns still jut from the podium today.)

The *Pantheon*, home of all the gods, is the Roman temple lionized by architects and visitors today. Designed by Hadrian and dedicated in the year 125, it set a new standard in construction and beauty. Brick and concrete combine to form the largest dome in the world. Its diameter of 43.3 meters is the same as its height, so that it would form a perfect circle if completed. As the interior curve of the dome moves upward, the coffered walls thin to relieve the weight. Seven ranks of pillowed rectangles decorate the interior dome, diminishing in size as they reach an open circle at the top. Suggesting the globe and the sun, the Pantheon emphasizes the interior (*cella*) rather than the exterior of the temple. Hadrian's design foreshadowed the future importance of churches, which would replace temples and which would also emphasize interior beauty.

By late August or September of 128 the restless emperor was back in his beloved Greece. He and Antinous were initiated into the highest level of the Great Mysteries of Eleusis. The 2000-year-old cult was thriving with members eager to find some answers to the questions of good and evil, life and death and human destiny. Greco-Roman gods could not do that.

The buildings that were begun on the emperor's earlier visit included a temple to Hera, an aqueduct and a gymnasium. He had also resumed construction on the Temple of Zeus Olympeion, which would be the focus of his panhellenic vision for Athens. Set in the valley beneath the Acropolis, it was built on a podium 135x354 feet. Its 104 pentelic columns soared 54 feet into space, framing a single cell. Dedicated to the father of Greek gods in 129, its cell contained a statue of Zeus over 35 feet high. (At least twelve of its fluted Corinthian columns remain.) Wealthy Greeks like Herodes Atticus imitated Hadrian's magnificence and magnanimity. He built the Odeion on the slopes of the Acropolis, its semicircular tiers of seats and stage fully restored today.

Hadrian consciously encouraged a cult to himself. The citizens of Athens erected the Arch of Hadrian (also still standing) to mark the entrance to his New City. He accepted the title Olympios from the Athenians and dedicated many altars and temples to himself as he traveled through Asia. This was the most prosperous part of the Hellenic world, and he would act magnanimously in his third visit there. He built baths and a *palaestra* (athletic field) at Miletus. In Athens he had listened attentively while Christians explained their beliefs. Now he would add the name Adriana to Tarsus, birthplace of Paul.

Reaching Antioch (*Antakya*) in June of 129, he felt misgivings about the frontier. To the east lay the polyglot regions and cultures that had clashed with the Greco-Roman civilization. The fanatical cults of Jews, Christians and the followers of Baal had never become assimilated. Hadrian respected differences, but the insistent exclusiveness of the Jewish religion and their separateness of race broke down the unity he so cherished. Still, he continued his journey into Cappadocia and Armenia. At Samosata (Samsat) he hosted a great *durbar* (formal reception), accepting and exchanging gifts with the client kings of the frontier and sealing his friendship with them. Though Chosroes did not attend, his daughter was at last returned to him.

On the way south, he stopped at *Berytus* (Beirut), the most Italian city of the Levant. With an excitement born of a fertile mind, he ordered the road running from there down to *Sidon* (Saida) rebuilt. Known as the Way of the Sea, it is said to be the oldest stretch of road in the world (Perowne: 131). Marching eastward, he visited Arabia (Trans-Jordan), the desert province carved out by Trajan.

Damascus, Palmyra and Petra were thriving crossroads cities of the caravan trade with Parthia, India and China. Hadrian renamed Petra Hadriana and commissioned a highway connecting Damascus with the desert cities of Bostra (Busra), Philadelphia (Amman), Hadriana and Aqaba on the Red Sea. Silks, spices and caged animals could now move more safely through the desert, which separated the far outposts of the Roman *fasces* (bundles of rods attached to a handle, they symbolized Roman power).

In Judaea in 130 (131?), Hadrian's decidedly anti-Jewish feelings led to three major edicts. First, he banned circumcision throughout the Empire, considering it an inhumane act. (For the same reason he had earlier forbidden castration of slaves.) Though he eased this ban for Egyptians, it was particularly offensive to the Jews, for whom it was a religious ritual. (It would be rescinded for the Jews by Antoninus.) Second, he decided to rebuild Jerusalem as a Roman colony. He would replace the old Jewish capital and bring in a large Greek population so that Jerusalem would become a Greco-Roman center. Third, on the site of the Temple of Jahweh he built an altar to Jupiter-Zeus.

Continuing his travels, it is possible he rode by horseback across the trackless Negev and Sinai deserts until he connected with the Nile coastal road that led to Pelusium. (He might have gone by sea, as the ladies in his retinue did.) There he rebuilt the tomb of Pompey the Great, who had lost his life in the East. At Alexandria he was electrified by the admiring crowds and the historical buildings. He built spacious temples and visited the tomb of Alexander the Great.

It was in September or October of the year 130 that Hadrian and his retinue set sail on a fateful trip up the Nile. Some days into the pleasant and relaxing voyage, Antinous, now eighteen to twenty years old, drowned. His body was recovered on the east bank of the river at a little village called Hir-wer. Not far away stood the ruins of the temple of Ramses II. On the opposite bank lay the city of Hermopolis.

Antinous became world-famous through his death. Hir-wer would be replaced by Antinoopolis. This memorial city marked the beginning of a cult that would spread throughout the Empire. (It was so endowed by Hadrian that Napoleon's surveyors estimated in the 1790s that some 1344 columns were still standing--just in the city center.) Many pilgrimages set out for shrines and temples dedicated to him. His image appeared on statues, brooches and coins. He was identified with the Egyptian god Osiris. Myth claimed that Osiris had died in the Nile, resurrected, and then brought fertility to the soil. The Greeks saw in him the god Dionysos. He, too, had suffered, died, been reborn and brought fertility. The images of the beautiful and sensitive Antinous were duplicated for a century and a half (even appearing again in Renaissance paintings).

While Christians and Jews were condemning it, Hadrian promoted the cult and named more cities after the youth. Antinous's birthplace of Bithynion had been renamed Claudiopolis a century before. Set amid the hills just thirty miles from the Black Sea, it had been an important link between East and West. On his earlier tour, Hadrian had returned to it its former name. Now he renamed it Bithynion Hadriana (Bolu or Boli).

The circumstances of Antinous's death remain "the longest and least conclusive inquest in history" (Perowne: 155). The most probable cause--between accident, murder and suicide--is that the youth sacrificed himself in the Nile as an offering to Hadrian. There was an ancient belief that anyone who drowned in the Nile would be deified. What greater glory might Antinous seek? The emperor had been ill, yet the best physicians had not been able to ease his pain. And one statue depicts Antinous with facial hair, evidence showing that his age was probably bringing his relationship with the emperor to an end. No greater act could the young lad have offered than his own life as a sacrifice to the health of the man with whom his life had been so totally intertwined.

Yet, the most revolutionary outcome of this cult worship would be its benefit to Christianity. By encouraging the worship of a mere human, Hadrian, as well as those people who followed any trend, reduced polytheism to the absurd. This turned some minds, at least, to accept the notion of monotheism. With the destruction of Jerusalem the emperor also assured that, as monotheism began to take root, it would be Christian and not Jewish (Perowne: 15).

How did those two religions find their separate identities within the Roman Empire? Judaism strove for the salvation of a people and race; Christianity taught the salvation of all individuals. Judaism promised a Messiah; Christianity knew the Savior. Judaism stressed a fearful, impersonal God; Christianity offered a loving, personal God. And the Mediterranean myths of Osiris, Dionysos and the hundreds of lesser gods? No one had ever seen them. But Jesus they saw, they lived with, they walked and talked with and listened to, and it made the difference.

Hadrian was back in Greece when the last Jewish rebellion flared up in 131. A fanatical Jew, Simon Bar Kokhba (Son of the Star), led the revolt first by seizing Jerusalem, then by restoring part of the Jewish temple. Bent on remaking Jerusalem as a Jewish city, he and his followers persecuted Christians, thus emphasizing their differences. When word of the uprising reached Hadrian, he returned to the region at once, with at least five legions and auxiliary forces in tow. It would be the only serious military operation of his reign.

By 134 Jerusalem was again a hill of rubble, its Jewish population nearly exterminated, though pockets of resistance continued until 136. It was at this time that the city was renamed Aelia Capitolina and designed as a Roman city, with its main street on a north-south axis (*cardo maximus*), as it is today. A magnificent port was ordered built, just north of Joppa (Tel Aviv) on the Mediterranean coast to service the province. Taking the name Caesarea Maritima, it became the capital and seemed to seal the fate of Judaea.

Hadrian returned to Rome about the year 135. There he might have been inspired first to offer sacrifice at the splendid Temple of Venus and Roma. He might then have sponsored a celebration, something he did only occasionally. Perhaps this was the time when he offered gladiatorial combats for six days. It is known also that he celebrated his birthday on one occasion by the slaughter of a thousand wild animals.

If his heart was heavy with the loss of his companion and growing health concerns, he could feel much satisfaction nevertheless. He had charmed Greece and the East; he had promoted the trendy cult of the deified Antinous; he had enriched the Empire with numerous roads, cities and buildings that had sprung up in his wake. He had also ended the Jewish rebellion.

Journeying to his villa, he viewed the exotic new *Nymphaeum* (large decorative fountain) and enjoyed the privacy of his surroundings at Tivoli. Still experiencing the nose-bleeding and high blood pressure that come with hardening of the arteries, he ordered construction of a *mausoleum* (large burial monument). If Augustus was buried beneath a *rotunda* (domed roof) near the Tiber, Hadrian, his admirer, would build an even larger memorial, and that is what he did. Designed with a rotunda set on an 84-meter-square foundation, it stands conspicuously on the Tiber's right bank. To reach it from the city, a stately bridge, the *Pons Aelius*, was built, lined with life-sized statues. (Its three original central arches still support the bridge.)

The rotunda itself, faced with marble and statues, measures 60 feet from base to summit. A ramp forms counterclockwise spirals till it reaches the top. There an opening leads to a room where the ashes of Hadrian, Sabina and their successors were laid to rest until the third century. (The massive mausoleum became a fortress during the Renaissance. Known today as the Castel Sant'Angelo, it houses a fabulous museum.)

About this same time the princeps ordered a new style of building at Ostia. The brick and concrete houses of two and three stories were innovations that gave evidence of an age of peace and prosperity. Staircases lead to open penthouses, which afford a view of gridiron streets, their rhythm broken by a forum, the temple of Zeus and the public baths, a center of comfort, exercise and cultural exchange. Wide windows also signaled a new urban style, and townhouses have a remarkably modern appearance. Though the harbor was often blocked by silt from the Tiber, Ostia was an important and wealthy center of commerce. The city appears quite cosmopolitan--a Jewish cemetery can even be found tucked away down a quiet side street.

Succession and Immortality

By the year 136 Hadrian's illness was confining him to painful spells in bed. He had no children, no close friends and no designated heir.

The Senate, always suspicious and never sympathetic toward this self-made man who rejected the experts, was scanning the horizon. Like buzzards at a deathwatch, they were looking for a successor.

Word reached the emperor, possibly through his spy system, that his aged brother-in-law Servianus wanted his grandson Fuscus to be named successor. Intolerant and aloof, Hadrian had both condemned without blinking an eye. The Senate was stunned into silence. It was also about this time that his wife Sabina died, though her departure was not felt as a crucial loss to the emperor.

Still, the question of succession remained. Hadrian's choice fell upon Lucius Ceionius Commodus Verus. A senator and friend, he was unpopular with both Senate and military, yet he was chosen and adopted with the name Lucius Aelius Caesar. From this time on, the name Caesar would be given to every emperor's adopted heir. Hadrian spent a fortune to win the support of the military and the Senate for his choice. It was all a waste. Aelius Caesar died abruptly on January 1st of 138, bringing on another crisis.

Another senator was named. Descendant of a Roman family from Gaul, T. Aurelius Arrius Antoninus, age 51, wealthy and virtuous, was granted the *imperium*. An old friend of Hadrian, he was without children. For this reason he was first required to adopt two successors named by Hadrian. The first of these was Marcus Annius Verus. A youth of seventeen, he was a nephew of Antoninus and a nephew of the emperor's wife Sabina. He would become the Emperor Marcus Aurelius. The second was Lucius Aelius Verus, the seven-year-old son of the deceased Aelius Caesar.

The succession was now in place, not for one but for two generations. Antoninus was left at Rome to deal with affairs of state. Meanwhile, the exhausted and suffering emperor decided to forsake his villa and journey to the thermal waters at Baiae on the Bay of Naples. There he called for magicians, but they could not relieve his pain. He begged his servants to kill him, but apparently they were stopped or ran away. They also disarmed him when he once reached for a dagger and put it to his throat. He pleaded with a doctor for poison, but the latter was so upset that he took some himself and died.

Antoninus arrived, perhaps summoned by the emperor, who was by this time on his deathbed. On the 10th of July in 138, Hadrian, the "second founder of Athens," died (Syme: 19). His urn was placed alongside his wife's in the still incomplete mausoleum on the Tiber. Antoninus moved quickly to persuade a reluctant Senate to deify him.

VII. Antoninus Pius

The transition from a high-profile emperor to the elegant ex-senator Antoninus, came easily for the Senate. They had feared Hadrian's impulsive behavior, especially upon his return to Rome to wind down his rule. There he had seemed like a stranger in their midst, and indeed, he had lived at Tivoli rather than on the Palatine. Now with his death the Senate was still cautious because of the soldiers, who revered his memory.

Antoninus had a good relationship with his colleagues in the Senate. He had followed in the footsteps of his father and grandfather, both of whom had been consuls. Their family had come from Nemausus (Nimes) in Gallia Narbonensis (southern France). Conquered by the Romans in the first century B.C., it was a rich agricultural region. The famous aqueduct there, known as the Pont du Gard, was built in the time of Augustus. Other imposing monuments to the vitality of the region include a temple, the "Maison Carree," and the amphitheater. (Dating from the late first or early second century, it is still used for bullfights.)

Youth and the Cursus Honorum

The future emperor Antoninus, after progressing through the *cursus honorum*, was appointed one of four consulars in Italy. He married Anna Galeria Faustina, the aunt of Aelius Verus. They had two sons and two daughters, but only the latter two survived their youth. The younger of these, Faustina, was born in 127. A year or so later the elder daughter died. That same year (128 or 129) Antoninus was named proconsul of Asia by Hadrian. There he ruled successfully and gained that layer of *auctoritas* (authority) that meant so much in Roman society. When his tour ended, he again took up residence at his villas at Lorium and Lanuvium. There he and his small family resumed their close friendship with Hadrian.

In 139 the newly crowned emperor Antoninus gave the title of Caesar to his heir, Marcus Annius Verus (Marcus Aurelius). Six years later he united his younger daughter Faustina in marriage with him. He followed this by giving his heir "proconsular imperium and tribunician power," officially confirming Hadrian's orders and strengthening the new dynasty of the Antonines. Marcus Aurelius now held Imperial authority outside Rome and was a junior partner in the government. Lucius Verus, the other adopted son, received no position at all.

As a person, Antoninus won the approval of all sectors of society. His habits were simple and moderate, his attitude congenial and accommodating. He acquired the name Pius during his very first year as emperor. His success in getting Hadrian deified, in opposition to the wishes of the Senate, reflected his piety (*pietas*), a strong sense of duty in both human and divine affairs. This is believed to be the reason why he was give his new name.

A Humane Administration

Though Antoninus reigned for twenty-three years, he was not viewed as a great statesman. He continued Hadrian's defensive frontier policy. His administrative changes seemed to be a step backward. Favoring the Senate, he ended the system of four judges for Italy. He kept provincial governors in their positions beyond their normal tour of duty.

He was careful about Imperial finances. Even though he reduced some taxes, the treasury held 2,700 million sesterces at his death. He did not imitate Hadrian in visiting the provinces, believing that the modest one, but the emperor was liberal in awarding nine congiaria. In 147 Rome celebrated the 900th anniversary of its founding. Antoninus had the pleasure of presiding over the *Ludi Seculares* (Secular Games) that year. In his generosity he contributed to the festivities by building a temple to Hadrian and completing his mausoleum.

No serious warfare took place during Antoninus's reign, except in Britain. With so many ethnic groups in the Empire, small-scale uprisings were common throughout Rome's history. In Britain the *Brigantes* tribe rebelled but was defeated in 140. This inspired a whole new line of forts. Consisting of a *fosse* (ditch) flanked by an earthen wall, the line ran thirty-seven miles through the countryside north of Hadrian's Wall. A military road was built with ten camps along the way, each surrounded with a mound and fosse. The Antonine Wall was a show of force and determination that led to sixty years of peace in Britain, but Antoninus's energetic policy was not matched on the Danube or in the East. There the Parthians were again stirring up trouble in Armenia. A small revolt broke out in Dacia and another in Egypt. The last probably brought Antoninus to the Nile in 154. Difficulties in the East were healed with temporary peace in 155 but war would come later.

More than anything else, the rule of Antoninus led to a spirit of humanity in Rome and the Empire. A sense of justice, rather than the letter of the law, began to take hold in the *basilicae* (law courts), as well as in senatorial rulings and within the villas of the ruling classes. Antoninus was responsible for this subtle change of spirit through his policies. He insisted that justice be applied equally to all. He tried to improve the condition of slaves. He softened the use of torture in questioning them; he stopped the use of torture for those under fourteen. In trials he insisted that the accused were innocent until proven guilty. Trials were to be held and punishments given where the crimes were committed. He also allowed Jews to resume their practice of circumcision.

Still, Antoninus upheld the social distinction between the *honestiores* (the better class) and *humiliores* (the poorer class). The criterion for these two divisions of society was wealth, and it resulted in different penalties for the same offense, a traditional Roman practice. The honestiores could neither be tortured, nor could they be executed by burning or being thrown to wild beasts.

Antoninus was a very religious man. Fulfilling his role as *Pontifex Maximus* (chief priest), he gave both public and private honor to the gods. He tolerated the many religions and sects of the Empire and discouraged persecution of Christians.

When Antoninus's wife Faustina died in 141, the emperor felt crushed. He promptly had her deified and commissioned a temple to her memory. Like his predecessors Nerva and Trajan, Antoninus made a new *alimentary* (food) donation for orphan girls, in honor of his wife. The young girls became known as *Faustinianae*. Because of Faustina's beauty, there had been lingering talk of scandal, but there was never any proof of her infidelity. Such talk was commonplace at all levels of society at that time, and the Imperial palace bore the brunt of human foibles.

Though Antoninus did not remarry, he had a concubine, a freedwoman who cared for him. His two adopted sons lived with him in the former home of Tiberius on the north slope of the Palatine. There he shunned formality and formal wear in daily affairs. For example, he wore a tunic at receptions instead of the toga. The one place where his weakness for luxury showed itself was in his staff. He had a servant just to announce visitors (*nomenclator*), another to keep silence among the slaves (*silentiarius*). Still another served as the teacher of the pages (*pedagogus puerorum*).

Death and Deification

Antoninus was fond of the countryside. He had been raised in the country and often left Rome for his villa at Lorium on the Via Aurelia, just to the north of Rome. There he loved to hunt and fish, or to read and write while enjoying the company of his younger daughter Faustina. There he fell ill and died on March 7, 161, at the age of seventy-four. He had developed a violent fever after eating some fresh cheese from Helvetia. The fever would not leave him. On his deathbed he recommended Marcus Aurelius as his successor but made no mention of Lucius Verus. He called his aides to his bedside. He then asked that the gold statue of Fortuna be moved from his bedroom to that of Marcus Aurelius. He commended the state and his daughter Faustina to Marcus.

Antoninus died beloved by all. He was a kind and gentle man, and mild of manner, yet robust and eager for the outdoors. Beyond this, he was prudent in behavior, moderate in all things, and always ready to sit and talk and listen. It was also said that he was "indifferent to the beauty of his slaves." The strength of his character and personality extended beyond his household, into the very attitudes of the citizens of the Empire. They began to see the human side of the law and to respect the differences among all men. A concern for the individual, as well as for the suffering sectors of society, was the mark left by Antoninus Pius upon the Roman Empire.

The Senate unanimously ordered a public funeral. The funeral pyre was set in the Campus Martius, the large field used for military training, which lay just outside the old city walls. Atop the pyramided form there was a statue of Antoninus standing in a chariot. The pyre was set on fire, and as it burned, an eagle was released in memory of the emperor, whose spirit now rose to the heavens, there to set amidst the galaxy of the gods.

The two adopted sons of Antoninus both offered orations in the Forum, and many gladiators met their death to celebrate his deification. The temple he had dedicated to his wife Faustina was not yet completed. The Senate, in a show of unity, voted to dedicate it to both Antoninus and Faustina. Today one can walk along the Via Sacra in the Forum and pause before the temple. Its classical columns soar skyward, ending in an ornate *architrave* (horizontal piece resting on the columns). There one can still read the dedication, sculpted in the frieze high above: *"Divo Antonino et Divae Faustinae ex. S.C."* ("to the deified Antoninus and the deified Faustina, by order of the Senate").

VIII. Marcus Aurelius

Though leaving the smoke and ashes of death behind, Marcus Aurelius felt the pain of any man who had lost his father. Almost from the day he was born, there was a bonding between him and his guardians. First it was his grandfather, then his predecessor and uncle, Antoninus. Marcus was raised in elite company. With famous tutors, he was destined to bring honor to the Empire as the last of the wise and "good emperors," as they were known to history.

Youth and Education

Marcus Aurelius was born at the villa of the Annius Verus family on the Caelian Hill in Rome on 26 April 121. According to custom, he received the *praenomen* (first name) Marcus on the ninth day after his birth. A distinguished family, the Annius Veruses were descendants of an Italian colony that had settled in Succubo, near Cordoba, in *Hispania Baetica* (southern Spain). When Marcus was born, his grandfather, M. Annius Verus, was serving as the *praefectus urbi* (prefect of Rome). He was also serving as consul for the second time that year, and had earlier been elevated to the patrician class by Vespasian. The infant's father, Annius Verus, had also twice served as consul. His great-grandfather had first emigrated to Rome, where he was appointed senator. His father had married a lady whose father had also twice served as consul. Her grandfather had also twice been consul and had held the reins of prefect of Rome. Her name was Domitia Lucilla, mother of Marcus. She was one of Rome's richest heiresses. Marcus Aurelius's aunt--his father's sister, Annia Galeria Faustina--would in the future marry Titus Aurelius Antoninus (Antoninus Pius).

Marcus was only a few months old when his father died. His grandfather then took the infant and raised him in his own villa on the Caelian Hill, near the villa where Marcus was born.

As a youth, Marcus had ideal living conditions. He loved to read and found much peace in walking among the gardens at his grandfather's villa. He grew up during the high tide of Greek influence at Rome. Hadrian's court was promoting the Athenian model for Roman students: *mens sana in corpore sano* (a sound mind in a sound body). Not surprisingly, Latin and Greek were now studied together at the *scolae* (schools) of the capital. The Greek language, literature, philosophy and medicine were making inroads at all levels of learning in the Western provinces. Marcus's mother spoke and wrote Greek fluently. It was fashionable then, and its impact has been felt in the West ever since. (Horace wrote that "Captive Greece took Rome captive.")

Roman education had always stressed character first. It encouraged simplicity and plain living at a time when wealth and social status held sway in the public mind. Domitia, too, stressed modesty of manners and enjoyment of nature, books and friendships that avoided luxury. Marcus loved his mother and liked to talk with her. He later claimed that he gained his respect for the poor through the long evening talks with Domitia Lucilla.

With high goals in mind, Marcus's grandfather and mother decided that the youth should study at home with tutors. Only the best were invited. One of these was Alexander of Cotiaeum. A famous Greek interpreter of Homer, he taught the youth to analyze the character of the gods. Were they wise and virtuous in their lives? Whose good were they interested in?

In his youth Marcus loved the manly sports of boxing, wrestling and running. From Diognetus he learned to be mentally and physically tough. He slept in a hard bed with few clothes. He grew patient with simple talk and began writing boyish dialogues. Diognetus taught him to avoid palmists and soothsayers.

- - - - -

Stoicism was a philosophy that taught strict discipline and self-control. Marcus was so attracted to it that it soon became his way of life. He matured fast and came to reflect a solemn (*gravis*) appearance early in his life. At age eleven or twelve he adopted the cloak of the philosophers and began to live only with the bare necessities. His mother finally convinced him not to sleep on the ground with just a cloak. He avoided excesses in the midst of his wealth and developed a distaste for the Colosseum, the Circus Maximus and even dramas.

On the eve of his fifteenth birthday (26 April 136) Marcus laid aside the symbols of youth, his *trabea* (youth's white toga with purple stripe) and golden amulet. It was time to don the *toga virilis* (toga of manhood). Emperor Hadrian betrothed the teenager to Ceionia Fabia, daughter of L. Ceionius Commodus, who was consul that year. At the same time, Ceionius Commodus was adopted by the emperor as the designated heir and given the name T. Aelius Caesar. It was the first time the heir apparent to the Empire would receive the name of Caesar. (Aelius was Hadrian's family name.) With that, the emperor-designate was sent to Pannonia.

Relationship with Hadrian

Emperor Hadrian was very ill by January 138 and was determined to ensure the continuity of the Empire by means of an adoptive son and heir. The connection between Hadrian and the young Marcus Aurelius went back to Marcus's youth. During those years, while he was still playing at the feet of his grandfather, the highly respected senator, Titus Aurelius Antoninus, would often stop to visit with Marcus's grandfather. The two shared views of the day's events in the Senate and the provinces. M. Annius Verus had just one daughter, Annia Galeria Faustina, the sister of Marcus's deceased father. The grandfather, no doubt after serious consideration, gave his daughter in marriage to Antoninus. This unknowingly set the stage for Hadrian's successors.

Hadrian, it must be recalled, was of Spanish origin, like M. Annius Verus. Both men had sprung from the ranks of provincial officer to the highest rungs of power. Hadrian was also a frequent visitor to the villa, where the two aging compatriots would sit and talk about earlier times. There the emperor would also meet and discuss affairs of state with the distinguished senator Antoninus, whom he respected. What the emperor especially admired about Annius Verus was that he had children. Hadrian had none. Little Marcus, the grandson, was a pleasant sight to the emperor, and each time the latter would say farewell to his aging pal and friend, he'd call out, "Educate him well." He liked to shower favors on the little child when he came to visit. He made him a member of the College of the Salii, an ancient religious priesthood, generally composed of older men.

In 127 their second child, Faustina, was born to Antoninus and Annia Galeria. A year or so later their elder daughter died. Antoninus was appointed by Hadrian at this time to serve as proconsul of Asia, and he and his family were away for two years. Upon their return to Rome in 130, they took up residence again at their favorite villas at Lorium and Lanuvium, renewing their personal friendship with the emperor.

Meanwhile, Marcus's grandfather had served his third consulship in 126. He blended his duties with a dedication to raising his grandson. It was he who made sure the best teachers were available to the child. When the grandfather died, ca. 129, Marcus and his mother moved to the home of Antoninus, who would continue to see to his nephew's schooling upon his return from Asia. The youth had an enviable time, studying with famous teachers, associating with political elites, talking with his mother and playing with his cousin Faustina.

He enjoyed a filial relationship with Antoninus. Thinking that Marcus read too much, Antoninus decided to get him out-of-doors. He gave the boy a pony and they'd ride together over the hills of Lorium before breakfast.

In 135 Hadrian returned from his long travels through the Empire and took up residence at his estate at Tivoli. His friendship with

Antoninus and his family continued. Two years later he appointed Marcus Aurelius, now sixteen, to be prefect of the annual Latin festivities at Rome. Marcus handled the responsibilities well. Then, on 25 February of 138, with the death of Aelius Caesar, heir apparent, Hadrian named Antoninus his new heir to the principate. The appointment was made on condition that Antoninus adopt both Lucius Ceionius Commodus, son of the deceased Aelius Caesar, and Marcus Aurelius. Thus, Hadrian had the satisfaction of naming not one but two future emperors. These arrangements assured the future stability of the Empire.

The choice of Antoninus to be Hadrian's immediate successor was a logical one. He was a mature man and popular in the Senate. He had been a member of Hadrian's council for some time. He would now begin to co-govern, and, when Hadrian died five months later at Baiae, he became sole emperor. Marcus Aurelius also got his first appointment from Hadrian to serve as quaestor. His duties were those of a private secretary, reading Imperial messages to the Senate.

When Hadrian died, Marcus Aurelius canceled his engagement to Ceionia Fabia and became engaged to his playmate and first cousin, Faustina the Younger. When Hadrian first made Marcus the adoptive son of Antoninus, it was with the understanding that he would give up plans to marry Faustina and that she should marry Lucius Verus. The problem ended with Hadrian's death because Marcus really wanted to marry Faustina, and Antoninus wanted him to. L. Verus, the other adoptive son, agreed to this. He was seven years younger than Faustina.

The Alter Ego of Antoninus

Marcus Aurelius began to serve as an *alter ego* (the other self) of Antoninus. In 139 he himself was named heir apparent and received the title of Caesar. Though he would not be given formal power (*imperium*) for six more years, he became an influential adviser to Antoninus. Antoninus rarely made appointments to public office without consulting Marcus. The two leaders worked so closely together that their administrations are called the "reign of the Antonines." Antoninus named himself consul for the third time in

139 and appointed Marcus Aurelius consul the following year.

A great celebration must have accompanied the marriage of Marcus Aurelius in 140 to Annia Galeria Faustina, daughter of the emperor, and his own first cousin. They eventually had thirteen children, yet only Commodus reached manhood. The others died in infancy except for one daughter. She married L. Verus and later was killed in Commodus's purge.

Antoninus had other reasons to be pleased that year, as the temple to the deified Hadrian was dedicated. It was his project. Also during this time, the emperor's protege continued his studies in rhetoric and language. Herodes Atticus, wealthiest of the Greek sophists, had come from Athens to be consul and to teach Greek oratory. He became Marcus's tutor.

Higher Education

Teachers of rhetoric had come from Spain during the Flavian era. The pendulum of culture had swung, though, and men of letters (*litterati*), like Annolius, Cyprian, Tertullian and Augustine were now coming increasingly from the provinces of Africa. Marcus Cornelius Fronto was one of these. Fronto was from Cirta in Numidia. Recognized as leader of Rome's legal eagles, he became Marcus's teacher of Latin and rhetoric, as well as his confidante.

During the second century, rhetoric had the reputation of being *regina artium* (queen of arts). It was supposed to produce the perfect man by aiming at flawless speech and writing, and was to help develop both charm and wit. Fronto's method of teaching was to write and receive letters from his pupils. His letters must have been brilliant, for he was often compared to Cicero. (And like Cicero's letters to friends, many of Fronto's letters to Marcus have survived.)

Marcus Aurelius, the Stoic philosopher, fond of the simple virtues, eventually rejected the rhetoric of Fronto. The two had purposes and styles that seemed to contradict each other. Marcus followed the beat of a different drummer. Now it was time to move on. He grew in modesty and discovered the writings of Epictetus, the Stoic philosopher (ca. 50-ca. 130), through his tutor, Q. Junius Rusticus. Apollonius of Chalcis taught him about free will and steadiness of purpose. He emphasized that reason was the highest form of truth.

Marcus continued to lead the lifestyle of a Stoic while fulfilling the duties of a Caesar. He kept up with the demands of his youthful position, growing daily in experience and responsibility, despite the fact that he was physically weak all his life. He was devoted to his mother, who lived with him and L. Verus in the palace of Antoninus and Faustina and their daughter. When Faustina died in 141, it was a time of great pain for Antoninus and his family. He dedicated a majestic temple to her in the Forum, where it has survived the centuries.

On the 10th of December in 146 Marcus Aurelius received the titles of *collega imperii* (colleague in command) and *consors tribunician potestatis* (partner in tribunician authority). From the Senate he received the *imperium extra urbem proconsulare* (proconsular power outside of Rome). This made him the second magistrate in Rome, "with supreme command of all her armies beyond the city frontiers." Marcus Aurelius was now jointly responsible with his father for the government of an empire.

The future emperor served three consulships during these formative years. It was while he was serving the third that Antoninus died (7 March 161). He was buried in Hadrian's mausoleum, begun by Hadrian but completed by Antoninus. The Senate quickly ratified Marcus Aurelius as sole princeps and accepted L. Verus as his colleague. The unique situation of having two "Augusti" presented no problem. L. Verus never dreamed of being emperor. He was always content with living a life of excesses and readily accepted the political leadership of Marcus Aurelius.

The Stoic Warrior

An uprising in Britannia posed the first major threat to the new emperor. Britannia had been a province since its southern tribes were subdued by Agricola in the year 84. Some forty years later, Hadrian's Wall was built to keep the barbarian tribes north of that imposing line.

Antoninus had extended the boundary farther north in 141 by building a rampart from the Forth (the River Bodotria) to the Clyde (the River Clote). (Both desolate boundaries are still visible.) The province below the boundary burst into rebellion when a legion under the leadership of Statius Priscus defied Rome's authority.

At the same time war erupted in the East when the Parthian king Vologaeses III invaded Armenia, destroying an entire legion. From there his forces entered Syria, in a bid to control the East. Marcus Aurelius got Senate approval for a war plan, and with that, an army marched eastward under the command of L. Verus.

The war lasted from autumn of 161 to the beginning of 166. Lucius Verus's generals, led by Avidius Cassius, directed the operation. The legions drove all the way to the Tigris river and into the kingdom of Media. By 163 Statius Priscus and his legions had regained Armenia, making it once again a client state. During the next two years he drove through the heart of Mesopotamia, capturing Seleucia and the Parthian capital of Ctesiphon. Suddenly disease struck the legions. As deadly as combat, it decimated the soldiers as they beat an orderly retreat back to the relative safety of the seacoast. Enroute, Roman bodies were strewn across the same desert that had witnessed the deaths of countless young legionaries before them. Unable to control the disease--smallpox?--the survivors brought it back to Rome, and from there it became the unwelcome visitor to every town and village across Europe.

Soon the Parthians regrouped and came storming back into southern Mesopotamia, while the Roman legions held tenaciously to the north. Then disaster struck directly at Rome. The Tiber recorded its worst ever flooding in 162, bringing in its wake a major famine.

The Barbarian Tribes

Though the emperor valued both his inner peace and the unity of the Empire, the struggle for that unity would take most of his life. Barbarian tribes posed the same threat that had vexed all emperors, and they were growing in numbers and power, step-by-step with the Empire. The defeat of one tribe simply created a void that was quickly filled by a waiting list of restless, aggressive, land-hungry, nomadic tribes that rushed to breach the gap in Roman resistance.

The causes of the security threat were as constant as they were unhealing. The Germanic tribes that had entered the region between the Rhine and Vistula continued to move about as they had done for centuries. Even after they finally began to settle down, the pressure upon them from eastern tribes continued. By the mid-second century they were so numerous that they could not produce enough food for their needs. They saw no alternative but to become active again. This time, though, they wanted to enlarge their lands, not simply wander and pillage. At the same time, the Ostrogoths, north of the Vistula, began to move toward the Black Sea. Though this time they would stop short of the Empire's boundaries, other tribes did not.

In 167 Roman officials received word that the Chatti were preparing for war and had already moved into Rhaetia (southern German-northern Swiss region). Then word came that the Marcomanni, the Quadi and the Iazyges, major tribes strewn all across the Danube, had invaded the Empire. They overran Noricum (Austria) and Pannonia (northern Yugoslavia-southern Hungary). The entire Danube area had become tempting since some legions had been withdrawn to quell the uprising in the East. From this time on, the Roman Empire would always be on the defensive, never again to enjoy the luxury of conquering new lands.

It was time for Marcus Aurelius to step up and lead. First, he needed funds. He began by auctioning some of the most revered treasures of the Imperial family. Then, by drafting mercenaries, slaves and even gladiators, he brought the legions to full strength.

The Roman army, with its standards aloft and banners fluttering in the breeze, filed past the gates of Janus, dogging the footsteps of Marcus Aurelius and Lucius Verus. All appeared highly motivated and well-equipped as they pursued the northern road that offered both adventure and danger. After a three-week trek of 300 miles they reached Aquilea in northern Italy. Only tribal chiefs met them there, and their only concern was to sue for peace. The main force of the tribes had broken up after some disputes. It had long been part of their character to fight among each other. They were warrior societies.

The emperor believed that the history of Rome's experience would repeat itself sooner or later. As he led the legions into Noricum and Pannonia, his objective was the total defeat of the restless tribes. Events seemed to go his way, for by the summer of 168 the Quadi were forced to sue for peace. This allowed the emperor and L. Verus to return to Rome for reinforcements, stopping off at Aquilea on 6 January 168. At Rome, the emperor set about raising more forces and funds and visiting with his young son Commodus, whom he had hardly gotten to know.

Yet, even while the legions were tied down in Pannonia, new war clouds were appearing along the Empire's *limites* (boundaries). The same Germanic tribes from the eastern Rhine and extending across Europe to southern Sarmatia (Russia) continued restless and unpredictable. The strongest of these were the Marcommanni and Quadi, both poised once again to strike across the Danube.

Setting out for Pannonia, the emperor was forced to bury his brother, L. Verus, along the way. He died of apoplexy near Venice in 169 and was deified at once. Once arrived in the Danube river region, the emperor held council. Sixteen legions and an equal number of auxiliaries were now assembled in Pannonia, a force of ca. 150,000 men.

The struggle for land, the seesaw battles and the broken treaties led the emperor to decide on a settlement. He made the momentous decision to allow the tribes eventually to settle within the Empire. He next raised the status of the provinces along the Danube. *Pannonia Inferior* (lower Pannonia) was raised to a consular province, as was *Pannonia Superior* (upper Pannonia). He replaced the procurator of Rhaetia with the legionary commander there, elevating him to governor of the province. The lines of fortresses were also strengthened.

With these administrative changes in place, he led his forces into Pannonia. By the end of 170 the Iazyges had been routed. In the summer of 172 the legions crossed the Danube and defeated both the Marcomanni and the Quadi in their own territory. By October the

Marcomanni and ten allied chiefs had sued for peace. (The Marcomanni settled in modern Bohemia, the Quadi in Moravia.) The tribes were forced to surrender captives and livestock and to offer military service to Rome. Another tribe, the Costoboci, from their homeland in Galicia, had invaded the Balkans as far south as Athens. They, too, were defeated. It seemed the end of the campaign trail had finally been reached.

With these triumphs the emperor returned to Rome in 174. The ever restless Quadi, though, soon assaulted the frontiers of civilization again. With Marcus Aurelius among the legions, a "miraculous victory" took place. The Quadi had surrounded the main force of legions, keeping them in the heat and without water for five days. Many writers of that time noted that the Melitene legion--all Christians--in what appeared their final moment of desperation, knelt down to pray. Shortly after this, the rains came pelting down amid thunder and lightning. The legions filled their helmets and shields, desperately watering themselves and their horses. This was followed by a violent hailstorm, which completely routed the enemy. Marcus Aurelius himself witnessed these events and renamed the legion the "Thundering Legion."

After this victory the focus of warfare shifted to lower Pannonia, where the Iazyges had revolted. This time they were totally defeated.

Before the emperor could implement his plan to allow the tribes to settle, a new flashpoint arose in the East. A rumor that the emperor was dead led Avidius Cassius, the Syrian commander, to declare himself emperor.

Marcus Aurelius prepared to take the field against Cassius. He first sent for his son Commodus, whom he had named the new Caesar. The emperor was concerned because he hardly knew his son. He had been away for so long, accompanied only by his wife during eight years of warfare (167-75). Now he wanted to give Commodus some public exposure, and from that time on the son accompanied his father everywhere.

When word reached Antioch that the legions under the emperor were marching toward the Levant (eastern Mediterranean), the Syrian legions quickly abandoned Cassius, and he was killed. It was while leaving there to return to Rome in 176 that the beloved wife of the emperor died. She had been known for her great beauty, but there was an intriguing side to the empress. The suspicion that she had somehow been party to the uprising of Cassius has never been resolved. Even the circumstances of her death remain a mystery.

At Rome, the emperor's victories were met with great celebrations. He awarded the legions with a *congiarium* (donative). His son Commodus erected a monument to his father. (It is known as the Aurelian Column today; it commemorates the eight years of Danubian warfare conducted by Marcus Aurelius.) The emperor at this time named his son Commodus the new Augustus, making him a co-equal in the Empire.

His plans to annex the lands of the Marcomanni and Sarmatians, as Trajan had done with Dacia, went unfulfilled. Under the terms of the treaty the Marcomanni were not allowed to cross the Danube and would be allowed to trade with the Roman Empire only at the will of the emperor. The Quadi were forbidden to trade with any other tribe. They were not to allow their neighbors, the Marcomanni and Iazyges, to cross through their territory.

Rome seemed ready for a period of calm when suddenly the peace was shattered again. Gallic tribes burst into rebellion in the north (177-80). Moorish horsemen rode against the desert legions in Mauritania. Marcomanni and Quadi once again struck across the Danube, in search of land, booty and, ironically, safety. Marcus Aurelius had no choice but to leave his family and return to the site of so many military campaigns. He never completed his final campaign, dying at Vindobona (Vienna) on 17 March 180.

Stoic Virtue

Marcus Aurelius was an idealist and self-starter who found himself denied the conditions he wanted to accomplish his goals as emperor. Yet, he was able to make time, even while engulfed in the heat of battle, to write his famous *Meditations*.

The *Meditations* were written at different periods during the last ten years of his life. Never intended for public reading, they reflected the private thoughts and concerns of a character "tender and strong . . . built from work and suffering and duty nobly achieved." They were written while he was working on military strategy in a combat zone. There he would issue orders in Latin by day. At night, though, he refocused his thoughts and listened to the voice within him. He wrote those reflections in Greek.

Books one, two and three are his personal convictions. His purpose in the rest of the books seemed to be a moral one, a mirror of his deepest beliefs. The second book was written while he was camped in Moravia in the territory of the Quadi. The third book was penned at Carnuntum (modern Petronell) and Haimbourg on the Danube in Noricum (Austria). He dwelt on the virtues of modesty and humility in the sixth book, as well as the heavy burden of his office. It is known that the ninth book was written in 174.

Much of his writing reflects the virtues of Christianity. Though the only mention of Christians appears in the eleventh book (ca. 177), some have asked why he didn't become Christian. Yet, to Marcus Aurelius, as to most men of his time, Jesus seemed but a very good man who for some reason was executed. Faith in Jesus, though, was spreading steadily, at first among the poor, gradually finding converts in all of society. Though Marcus Aurelius was poor in spirit, he was not destined to be the first emperor to receive the faith.

Persecutions of Christians were largely local during the first two centuries of the Roman Empire. Two periods of persecution broke out during the Aurelian years. The first of these was suppressed in 166. In a famous case, Justin Martyr and about six others were whipped and then executed. Peace followed until 177, when some disturbances in Gaul led to a search there for Christians. Potruvius, a disciple of Polycarp, met his fate, as did other Easterners who had brought Christianity to Gaul. Some of these were cruelly executed. The emperor's position was to order those who abandoned Christianity to be freed. He generally tried to lessen the sufferings of Christians. As time went by, Christians lived in less and less danger.

Marcus Aurelius never came to grips with Christianity. He could not even believe in a separate existence after death. As a Stoic he had to deny the natural impulse to believe in a hereafter. To him it was but an irrational appetite. Unlike earlier writers--Cicero and Plutarch were examples--the emperor simply rejected all such natural feelings in his one-sided commitment to reason and logic. The writings of Aristotle offer six strong arguments for the existence of God. Evidently these were not read or studied by this intellectual ruler. Still, there is evidence that he struggled with the possibility of a hereafter.

The religion of Rome had never demanded that its citizens believe in a hereafter. Nor did it teach morals. Its main characteristic was to be correct and regular in its ceremonies. In that it was demanding. "To desert the ancient gods was to cut oneself off from Roman society, as the Christians were made to feel" (Dill: 544). If Rome and the Empire had no moral code outside their law courts, how could Marcus Aurelius or any emperor expect to give moral leadership? He was able to do it both by the force of his position and of his lifestyle.

Though the emperor was a Stoic and the citizens honored many gods, three separate gods of the East grew important during the first to the third centuries A.D. Isis and Serapis of Egypt and Mithra from Persia all had one thing in common: their followers believed in a life after death. And those gods made their followers tend to be monotheists. They wanted total acceptance by their followers, as well as total dedication. A belief in one God, then, was an undercurrent of the times. It paved the way for Christianity, which would soon sweep over the Empire. It was a more reasonable conclusion than the opposite, which Marcus Aurelius clung to.

To the Stoic, the voice of the God in his breast was the voice he followed. "He is truly learned that does God's will." The emperor listened to this voice. The key to his life was his resignation to this voice. It was clear in the logic he followed in pursuit of good, as well as his self-denial, where feelings clashed with logic. For Marcus Aurelius, as for any Stoic, reason eclipsed all other motives and was the supreme law of living. He must have feared no battle. Nor could he hesitate to do what he thought was right. Still, no one's feelings are perfectly obedient to logic.

Influence on Daily Life

The emperor also influenced daily life in the Empire. It had become a fact of life that the emperor alone had judicial authority in the Empire. In the case of Marcus Aurelius, he was zealous in the pursuit of justice for all his subjects. The praetors, aediles and local magistrates who ruled on court cases all enjoyed authority delegated by him. He heard only special cases at Rome, dedicating about eight months of the year to hearing and judging on them. Nor did he allow technicalities to interfere with the flow of justice.

He adopted Hadrian's system of judgeships for Italy but increased the number to five. Each judge was also made a praetorian (*iuridicus*), thus raising the five Italian judges to the same level they enjoyed in each province. They held the power to influence municipal authorities. At the town level magistrates referred cases exceeding a certain value to the iuridici. They, in turn, referred the most important questions to the emperor. This system, which he strengthened, lasted until the end of the third century, a tribute to its success.

On the domestic front, his principate emphasized freedom. He issued laws to touch the lives of slaves and women. Often masters made a contract with their slaves stating that if they performed certain tasks by a certain time, they would be freed. Often they broke the contract. The emperor made it illegal for masters to evade this contract, once set. If the slave had not yet fulfilled his terms, he still gained his freedom, though an official was appointed to make sure he completed the contract. The emperor also issued a law forbidding masters to sell slaves to fight wild animals in the arenas of the Empire. He often drafted gladiators into the legions, where they could gain freedom.

The emperor attempted to improve society by enforcing laws on family matters rather than by passing new ones. Wives at this time were mere property, just like a man's daughter. Marriages could be ended without public authority. Divorce was not well defined. As a result, family life and open adultery were hardly different. Public morals were not at a high level, and the legitimate and freeborn population was lessened. He prohibited marriage between a tutor and his pupil. No senator's daughter was allowed to marry her father's freedman. The purpose of this was to encourage the growth of the best families and improve society. The emperor encouraged the marriage of soldiers, too.

The issue of wills had been of much concern for years. Marcus Aurelius emphasized the intention of the testator in writing his will rather than the strictly legal form of the document. This improvement reflected the emperor's conviction that personal intention was more important than technical flaws. These rulings and interpretations were echoes of an emperor who raised the moral level of society by following the voice of God within him.

Though Marcus Aurelius did not believe in a hereafter, his moral standards left many Christians in admiration of his lifestyle. At his death the Empire lost its last stable and effective emperor for a century to come. And pagan Rome would continue to clash with Christian morality for two centuries to come.

End of an Era

Marcus Aurelius's son Commodus became emperor at his father's death. He proved an unworthy princeps, yet his father believed he had no other choice but to designate Commodus. One author stated the case best when he wrote that Commodus (180-92) was "one of the few Roman emperors of whom nothing good can be said" (Boak & Sinnigen: 335). He was the only natural son of an emperor to survive in almost a century. It would have appeared detestable for Marcus Aurelius to have murdered his son, even though he considered him a poor choice to rule. There was no other alternative than for Commodus to succeed his father.

When he was finally assassinated in 192, he was succeeded by Pertinax (192-93) and Julian (193). They proved equally inept, and the year 193, like 69, hosted a succession of four emperors, each supported by his fiercely loyal army. With the death of the last of the "good emperors," the Age of the Antonines had ended.

EPILOGUE

1. The Fall of Rome

From the end of the second century through the third century the Roman Empire saw a crumbling from within. The question of succession was the most serious of the factors that led to a weakening of government. It had never been settled to the satisfaction of all. First, blood lines, aided by adoptions, dictated the leadership of the Empire (Julio-Claudians). Second, civil war and the raw bid for power delivered the *Imperium* to the strongest (the Flavian Dynasty). Third, a series of adoptions led to the peaceful succession of five emperors (the five good emperors). After that the greater good of the Empire took second place to the power struggle among military commanders. They seized control with the support of legions that declared for one or another general, depending on what each legion saw as its own best interests.

With the head weakened, the body of the Empire seemed a tempting target. Old border enemies renewed their wars against the short-sighted giant, its head too large for its members: Parthians rose in the East (195), Caledonians in Britain (208), war resumed with Persia (230-233) and then on the Rhine frontier (234). Goths invaded Dacia and the Balkans in 238 and Lower Moesia (eastern Bulgaria) in 251. Perhaps the greatest humbling came when Emperor Valerian was defeated and captured by the Persians (259), then executed.

Though these border wars were severe, Rome was also besieged by

127

internal rebellion. Postumus tried to make Gaul a separate empire (258). The desert metropolis of Palmyra revolted (271), only to be reconquered (272), followed by the recovery of Gaul and Britain (274). Another tribal revolt in Britain (286) took a decade to suppress.

Time was no longer on the Romans' side. Border wars and internal revolts reflected the lack of attention given not only to leadership but also to the pressing needs of the masses. Land, especially in the West, came to be held in large tracts by the few. The land owners in Italy produced cash crops like grapes and olives. These fetched good prices in the form of wine and oil. Still, the production of wheat, the dietary staple, declined. This forced Rome to import more wheat from Egypt and Africa. Demand exceeded supply, and the inflationary spiral slowly reduced the peasant farmers to serfs. The economy also slowed down because of the scarcity of booty and the increase in taxes. Taxes were needed to fight holding actions on the borders and to put down ethnic rebellions, both largely motivated by a weak economy. A vicious cycle of taxation, inflation, hunger and rebellion formed a merry-go-round spinning toward disaster.

The worst was yet to come. The map of Europe and Asia beyond Rome's reach was fluid and violent. Tribes to the north of the Danube and east of the Rhine had prospered for centuries. They had grown large and powerful and had profited with long contacts at Rome's borders. Their men had been conscripted into the Roman legions from the second to the fourth centuries. The lure of army life among the Empire's citizens had given way to civilian life. This change in attitude came in part because the conquest of new territory with its promise of booty had ended. Emperors had also allowed and encouraged intermarriage between Roman garrisons and the native people. By welcoming these noncitizens into the army, emperors co-opted the threat of hostile tribes on the borders. Even during Nero's reign, 100,000 tribesmen, with their wives and children, had settled on the south bank of the Danube in Moesia. The Roman legions were becoming foreign legions. Though the soldiers' hands held the Roman *fasces* (insignia), their hearts kept faith with the polyglot of tribes from which they came. Their tribal headmen, their relatives, and the very towns and cities they were occupying required personal relationships far stronger than what a distant emperor might supply.

It is no wonder that, as tribes became stronger, and as the Empire aged, the Alemanni revolted (357), war with Persia returned (359) and the Visigoths crossed the Danube (376). Because Rome could not oust them, they were settled in Moesia (380-382). Then Alaric and the Visigoths, though stopped in Greece (396), made good the invasion of Italy (408).

Three large barbarian tribes now invaded Spain, the Vandals, the Sueves and the Alans (409), but this was just the beginning. Hopelessly on the defensive, the legions fought back. It would be an exercise in futility: the Visigoths captured the once proud Rome (410). They poured across the impregnable Rhine border into Gaul (412), and then into Spain (415). The Vandals moved from Spain into Africa's rich coastal provinces (429) after the Romans used the Visigoths to drive them out.

Large tribal attacks continued to spread south into the western provinces of the Empire. Hordes of infantry and cavalry, sometimes as many as 80,000, settled in less occupied provinces. Ostrogoths settled at first in Pannonia (454), while Vandals recrossed the Mediterranean from Africa and sacked Rome itself (455). For a time Rome had no emperor (465-467). In 472 the Visigoths again ransacked Rome.

Germanic tribes like the Heruli and Sciri were also plundering Italy. Led by Odoacer, they demanded land. When it was refused them, they killed Orestes, commander of the Roman soldiers and father of the last emperor, Romulus Augustulus. He now abdicated the throne (476) and Odoacer made himself king, granting his soldiers the land they craved in Italy. The western Empire was at last completely in barbarian hands.

From within, the question of succession, together with a neglect of agriculture and human needs, worked like a virus to weaken the State. Political, economic and social weaknesses drew down the quality of life for Rome and its western provinces.

From without, the growth of tribes and their cultures led inevitably to a clash with Rome. Rome's commitment to client-kingdoms was not strong enough to buy loyalty from those who saw the Roman Empire as the most desirable place to plunder, if not also to live. The very auxiliary forces that aided Rome gradually became a factor in support of the side they chose to take when the chips were down. Borders loosened and skills transferred. The temper of the citizens, once willing to serve in the legions and give their lives in defense of the "Senate and People of Rome," had drifted away. The civic spirit that found pride in the *mos maiorum*, the ancient values, good government and respect for law was exchanged for self-interest by the elites and the need for survival by the masses. The illiterate masses, once fed at Rome, were now cut from relief. They knew not where to turn. And their numbers increased far more rapidly than those who might have been able to change.

Still, the Roman Empire, during its first two centuries, had been ruled by a patrician class in support of a nearly absolute emperor. If attention had been given at that early stage to developing broadly educated masses, perhaps another Republic would have grown out of Rome's Empire. It is pure speculation. No educational system existed because there was very little need to read and a very great need to build.

The feeling of belonging had extended across the Empire -- all provincials were granted citizenship in 212. Still, the intercultural unity also allowed people to think that citizenship alone gave benefit. Where were those willing to speak up on behalf of citizen needs? Where were the leaders of the upper classes, who would criticize the Imperial court?

Rome's Empire relied from the start on the most powerful military leader. It was fortunate to have enjoyed many great leaders. It could not last. The military sub-culture became so glorified an element in society that it eventually swallowed that society. It drained the economy while it drew the civic spirit into a false sense of security. It discouraged the educated class from a leadership role. They had grown affluent in Rome and the provinces and gradually chose to devote their energy to the prosperity of their villas. The spirit of deterioration filtered into the military itself, which now was confronted with the mightiest opposition it had ever faced. It could not muster enough inner strength. It could not see its own weaknesses. It could only absorb the enemy, hoping it would be satisfied with violating the borders. Permission to stay was granted to the trespassers. At last, sheer numbers of tribes slowly drained the spirit of resistance.

If it is true of Rome's glory that *non fecit taliter omni nationi* -- "He did not do so much for every nation" -- it must also be true that *omnia tendunt naturaliter in non esse* -- "all things tend naturally toward disintegration." The Romans failed to address this dictum. It gradually swept away an Empire.

2. The Eastern Empire

The development of eastern and western branches of the Empire was a gradual process. Eastern cities had grown prosperous during the first two centuries of the Empire. They dated from earlier civilizations and had enjoyed long years of trade and development. Cultural differences, coupled with distances from Rome, slowly marked a cleavage between those provinces eastward and westward of Greece. The Latin language had become to the West what the Greek language had been to the East.

Recognizing this, Emperor Diocletian in 293 set up a four-man system to rule the Empire. Known as the tetrarchy, it had two Caesars, one for the East and one for the West. Each served under an Augustus and was the heir-apparent. The tetrarchy lasted until 312, giving a needed period of stability to the Empire.

A major step in the breakup of the Empire came early in the fourth century. Constantine became the new emperor after the battle of the Mulvian Bridge (*Pons Mulvius*) at Rome in 312. Inspired by a dream about Christianity, he ordered his legions to paint their shields with crosses. In the ensuing battle, he defeated his rival, Maxentius. Following his victory he signed the Edict of Milan (313), allowing Christians for the first time to enjoy freedom of worship.

With a sense of the future, Constantine decided to build a new capital in the East. There he would create a city that would not only rival

Rome; its splendor would surpass Rome's, which had already stood for a thousand years.

Constantine chose the site of ancient Byzantium for his capital. Located on a spit of land that all but joins Europe with Asia, he named his masterpiece Constantinople.

When completed (324-330), Constantinople became in effect a second Rome. Because it was in the more prosperous East, emperors at Constantinople were able to keep government, economy and society together. Barbarian tribes were attracted to Rome and the West. They did little to upset civilization in the East. By the time Rome fell in 476, Constantinople was a thriving capital. It would survive the destruction of Rome and the West.

The major roads of the East converged upon the walled city, with its Christian temples, its fine palaces, the Curia, the public Baths, the Hippodrome and aqueducts. All the glory that had once been Rome's was there, until it, too, yielded to conquest in 1453.

With the fall of Constantinople, Moscow would claim leadership of the Christian Orthodox religion under the title of the Third Rome. It would continue where Constantinople left off, serving as the beacon of civilization for several centuries, until it, too, succumbed.

Like rays of sunlight, the distilled learning at Constantinople carried across the mountains to Greece and the islands of the Aegean Sea. Spreading northward to Thrace, it extended to the Danube river region. From Asia (Turkey) eastward, the light of learning and the lamp of government and Christianity followed the old caravan trails, both ancient and modern, into Syria, Lebanon, Palestine and Jordan. Its civilizing mission was even borne on sailing ships up the Nile river and across Africa as far west as Cyrene.

Justinian, the most distinguished of the eastern emperors (518-565), gave strong support to Christianity, the new state religion. He ordered the rebuilding (532-537) of the famous Church of the Holy Wisdom (St. Sophia). He had experts summarize the old Roman laws. The *Corpus Iuris Civilis*--the Code of Justinian--was first published in 529. The Code became the sole law of the Empire. Since it was the only official textbook in the law schools of the Empire, whether a student chose to study at Rome, Constantinople or Beirut, his diploma mirrored a thousand years of law and order. Justinian is remembered also for his reconquest of some of the western provinces, including Italy, Dalmatia, western Africa and southern Spain.

3. Western Christianity

From the time of Constantine I's victory in 312, Christianity was allowed to practice openly in the Empire. It flourished alongside the pagan cults throughout the fourth century. Constantine helped settle differences among Christian leaders and led many of the upper classes to convert to the new religion.

Under the reign of Theodosius I (359-395), Christianity became not only the official religion of the Empire but also the trendy religion among those who counted throughout the fourth century. Theodosius even ordered his subjects in the East to accept Christianity (380). When he ordered the temple of Serapis in Alexandria destroyed (391), paganism was on its way out in the East.

Though the Christian bishop of Rome--the pope--was the head of Christianity, a rivalry developed with the bishop of Constantinople. The latter was recognized as the eastern leader and second only to the pope. The rivalry would continue to emphasize the differences between the eastern and western worlds. In the tenth century the bishop of Constantinople declared himself the head of Christianity in the East. It represented the maturing of a cultural split that had been festering within the Empire for a thousand years. Its roots in fact went back to the conquest of the eastern world by Alexander the Great.

As Christian leaders--bishops and priests--became a force for change in the West, they were given governmental authority in the towns and villages. There they were especially protective of the poor. As the barbarian tribal leaders replaced the Roman government, the clergy continued their support of the people against the barbarians.

Able leaders joined the educated clergy and donated land and money for the Church. The growth of monasteries reflected the development of the voluntary choice of Christianity as a total way of life. Pagan temples were routinely converted into the first churches. (Pagan temples with Christian decor can be visited in every town of Italy.) The flowering of Christianity through a personal God, a moral code, churches and the priesthood also hurried the end of the Roman Empire. Christianity called for new loyalties, fresh entertainments, a changed work week, and moral values. *In medio stat virtus* -- "virtue lies in the middle" -- became the new code word, and the *crucifix* replaced the *fasces* as the symbol of power. The old virtues of piety, dignity and fortitude were now reflected in Christian leadership. The persecuted Church had become the most stabilizing force and amazing success story to issue from the Roman Empire's collapse.

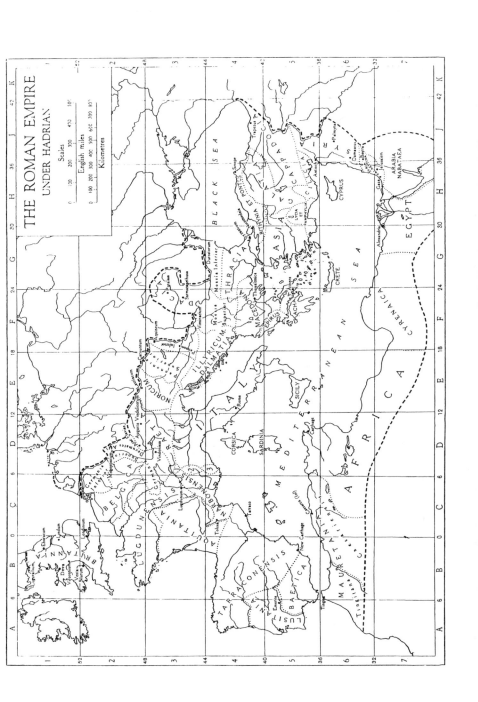

THE ROMAN EMPIRE
UNDER HADRIAN

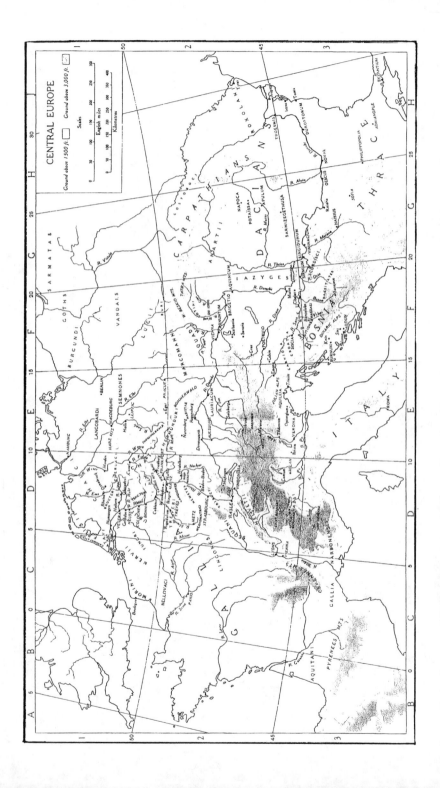

CENTRAL EUROPE

Ground above 1500 ft. ☐ Ground above 3,000 ft. ▦

Scales

English miles
0   50   100   150   200   250   300

Kilometres
0   50   100   150   200   250   300   350   400

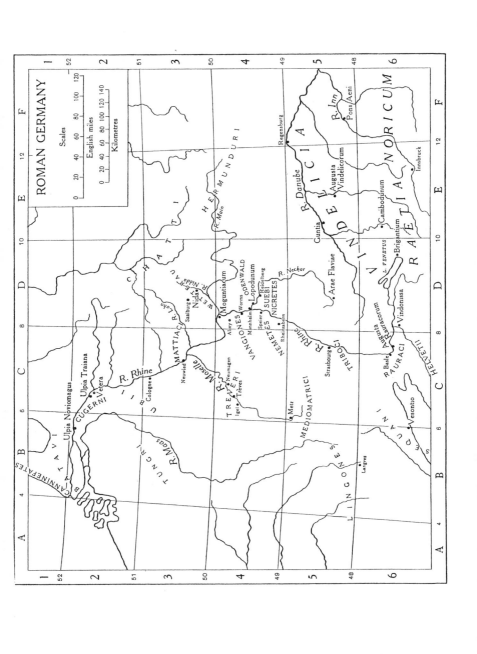

ROMAN GERMANY

Scales

English miles
0 20 40 60 80 100 120 140
Kilometres
0 20 40 60 80 100 120

CANNINEFATES

BATAVI

TUNGRI

Ulpia Noviomagus
Ulpia Traiana
CUGERNI
Vetera

R. Rhine

Cologne

R. Maas

R. Moselle

Neuwied

TREVERI
Igel
Trèves
Neumagen

MEDIOMATRICI

Metz

LINGONES

Langres

SEQUANI

Vesontio

HELVETII

R. Basle
Augusta
Rauracorum
AURACI
Vindonissa

TRIBOCI

Strasbourg

NEMETES
Rheinzabern
Speier
SUEBI
NICRETES

VANGIONES
Worms
Mannheim
Heidelberg
Lopodunum
ODENWALD

R. Neckar

Arae Flaviae

Vindonissa

Cambodunum

Brigantium

L. VENETUS

Innsbruck

RAETIA

NORICUM

VINDELICIA

Augusta
Vindelicorum

Pons Aeni
R. Inn

Regensburg

R. Danube

Guntia

MATTIACI

Saalburg
Nida
R. Nidda
WETTERAU
Moguntiacum

R. Lahn

TAUNUS

CHATTI

HERMUNDURI

R. Main

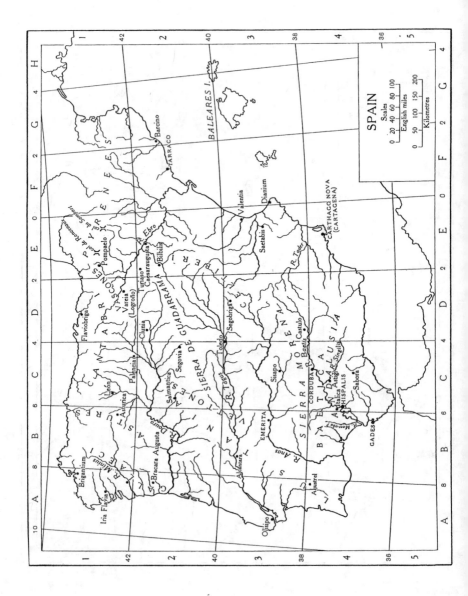

SPAIN

Scales
English miles
0   20 40 60 80 100

Kilometres
0   50 100 150 200

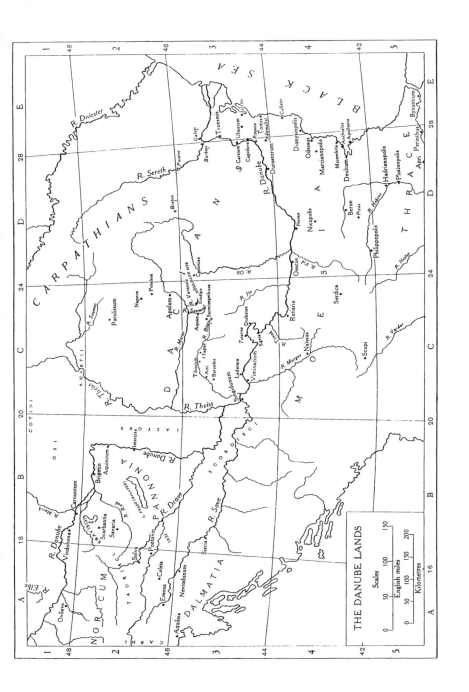

THE DANUBE LANDS

Scales

English miles
0   50   100   150

Kilometres
0   50   100   150   200

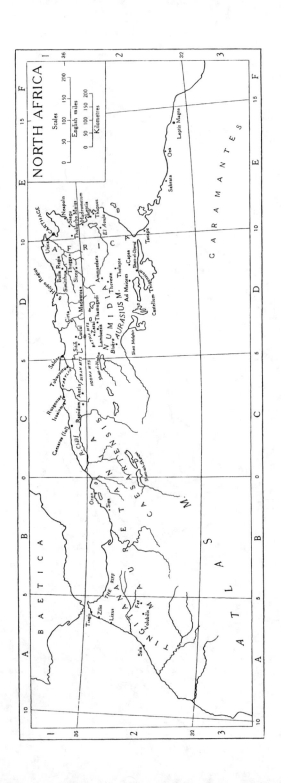

NORTH AFRICA

The Emperors of the Roman Empire

Augustus	27 BC-AD 14		Gordian III	238-44
Tiberius	14-37		Philip	244-49
Gaius	37-41		Decius	249-51
Claudius	41-54		Gallus	251-53
Nero	54-68		Aemilianus	253
Galba	68		Valerian	253-60
Otho	69		Gallienus	253-68
Vitellius	69		Claudius II	
Vespasian	69-79		Gothicus	268-70
Titus	79-81		Quintillus	270
Domitian	81-96		Aurelian	270-75
Nerva	96-98		Tacitus	275-76
Trajan	98-117		Florianus	276
Hadrian	117-38		Probus	276-82
Antoninus Pius	138-61		Carus	282-83
Marcus			Numerianus	283-84
Aurelius	161-80		Carinus	283-85
Lucius Verus	161-69		Diocletian	284-305
Commodus	180-92		Maximian	286-305
Pertinax	193		Constantius	305-06
Didius Julianus	193		Galerius	305-11
Septimius			Severus	306-07
Severus	193-211		Licinius	308-24
Caracalla	211-17		Maximinus Daia	310-13
Macrinus	217-18		Constantine	306-37
Elagabalus	218-22		Constantine II	337-40
Severus			Constans	337-50
Alexander	222-35		Constantius	337-61
Maximinus	235-38		Magnentius	350-53
Gordian I and II	238		Julian	361-63
Balbinus and			Jovian	363-64
Pupienus	238			

WEST   # EAST

Valentinian I	364-75	Valens	364-78
Gratian	367-83	Theodosius I	379-95
Valentinian II	383-92		
Eugenius	392-94		
Theodosius I	394-95		
Honorius	395-423	Arcadius	395-408
Valentinian III	425-55	Theodosius II	408-50
Maximus	455-57	Marcian	450-57
Majorian	457-61	Leo I	457-74
Severus	461-67		
Anthemius	467-72		
Olybrius	472-73		
Glycerius	473-74	Leo II	474
Julius Nepos	474-75	Zeno	474-91
Romulus			
Augustulus	475-76		
(Odoacer)	476-93		

Taken from Chester G. Starr's
The Roman Empire, 27 B.C. - A.D. 1982.
Courtesy of Oxford University Press, New York.

GLOSSARY

Terms and Phrases

ab urbe condita - a.u.c. - (date) from the founding of Rome
ad hoc - for this purpose
advocati fisci - a team of prosecuting attorneys for the state
    treasury
aedile - officer in charge of streets, public property and the
    grain supply
aerarium - senatorial treasury
Agri Decumates - the Rhine-Danube frontier; today the Schwarzwald
    and Odenwald in Southwestern Germany
alimenta - financial subsidies for poor children
alimentary - food (donation for orphan girls)
alter ego - the other self
amici - friends
Amphitheatrum Flavium - the Flavian Amphitheater (the Colosseum)
Anio Novus - Roman aqueduct built by Claudius
Antakya - Antioch, Syria
Antium - Anzio, Italy
Aqua Claudia - Roman aqueduct built by Claudius
Aqua Traiana - the last Roman aqueduct, near Lake Sabatinus
Aqua Virgo - Roman aqueduct built by Agrippa
aqueduct - elevated water supply system
aquiline - a hooked nose
Aquincum - Budapest, Hungary

137

Ara Pacis Augustae - Altar of Augustan Peace
architrave - horizontal piece resting on top of the columns
arena - sand
arx Albina - the Alban citadel of Domitian
auctoritas - authority derived from virtue
Augustus - Revered
aula - Imperial court, hall
Baetica - a southern province of Spain
basilicae - law courts
Berytus - Beirut, Lebanon
bete noire - person or thing strongly detested or avoided
Bibliotheca Ulpia - Greek and Latin libraries of Trajan
bona vacantia - property of those who died without wills or heirs
Britannia - Britain
caligula - literally, "Little Boot," from which the Emperor
    Caligula was named
Campus Martius - Field of Mars (Rome)
Camulodunum - Colchester, England
canabae - booths or settlements outside camps
Canopus - large rectangular pool with statues of gods, columns
    and arches at Hadrian's villa at Tivoli, near Rome
Capitolium - the first temple at Rome: so-called because it was
    built atop the Capitoline Hill (509 B.C.)
Capreae - the island of Capri, Italy
carceres - stalls for horses at the racetrack
cardo maximus - main street of a Roman city on a north-south axis
carpe diem! - "seize the day"
carpe momentum! - "seize the momentum" (--the author)
Casperius - Caspinus Aelianus
Castra Regina - Regensburg, Germany
cella - cell
censor - the census official; reviewed qualifications for
    senators and other positions by keeping property lists
censor perpetuus - censor for life
Circus Maximus - the main race course of Imperial Rome
civilitas - decency
cohort - a division of the Praetorian Guards; consisted of 480
    men
Colossus - a 99-foot-high statue of Nero
collega imperii - colleague in command

collegia iuvenum - military academies
comitatus - (an emperor's) retinue
comites - Imperial retinue
Concordia Exercituum - the harmony of the army
congiaria - public handouts of grain, dole (pl. of congiarium)
congiarium - a donative, bonus
consiliarii Augusti - permanent legal advisers made up of
    senators and equestrians
consilium - council
consilium principis - legal advisers
consors tribuniciae potestatis - partner in tribunician authority
constitutiones principum - Roman statutes, a source of law
Corpus Iuris Civilis - the code of Justinian
corrector reipublicae - special provincial administrator
crucifix - cross with the figure of Jesus crucified on it
Ctesiphon - Parthian capital on the Tigris river
curator reipublicae - special administrator, fiscal agent
curatores restituendae Campaniae - curators for the restoration
    of Campania
curia - the Senate House
cursus honorum - political career ladder
cursus publicus - the postal system
Dacia - Romania
Dalmatia - the eastern Adriatic coast; today it includes Croatia,
    Montenegro and Slovenia
damnatio memoriae - removal from all records
decemviri - a standing committee comprised of senators and
    community leaders
de facto - actual, in fact
de jure - legal, by law
delatores - informers
denarius - a silver coin, first minted ca. 211 BC
Diaspora - Dispersion
dignitas - dignity
Divi Vespasiani - Titus' temple to the deified Vespasian
"Divo Antonino et Divae Faustinae ex. S.C." - "to the deified
    Antoninus and the deified Faustina, by order of the Senate"
dominus - lord, master
Domus Aurea - Golden House of Nero
durbar - formal reception (Hindu)

edictum perpetuum - an edict made part of Roman law
equites - equestrians, the second order of Roman society
equites singulares - bodyguards from the cavalry
fasces - symbol of Roman power, bundles of rods attached to an
    axe handle
Faustinianae - orphan girls named after Antoninus's deceased wife
    Faustina
Festina lente! - "make haste, slowly!" (--Augustus)
fides - loyalty
fides commissa - wills with third parties
fiscus - Imperial treasury
fiscus Iudaicus - punitive tax imposed on Jews
fora - forums (pl. of forum)
forum - the center of urban activity and location of major public
    buildings
Forum Traianum - Forum of Trajan
fosses - ditches
frumentarii - couriers
Gallia - Gaul (France)
Gemoniae - the Stairs of Groans (Rome)
gens - family
Germania - Germany
gravis - a solemn appearance
gravitas - dignity
Hadriatic Sea - Adriatic Sea
haruspex - diviner of future events through reading of a liver
Hispalis - Seville, Spain
Hispania - Spain
Hispania Baetica - southern Spain
honestiores - the better class
hostis publicus - public enemy
humiliores - the poorer class
iecur - liver
Illyricum - (former) Yugoslavia
imperator - emperor
imperium - absolute formal power
imperium extra urbem proconsulare - proconsular power outside of
    Rome
in medio stat virtus - "virtue lies in the middle"
incestum - incest

intra cubiculum principis - in the privacy of the emperor's inner
  chambers
iuridici - assistants to the governors
iuridicus consularis - a judge of consular rank
ius respondendi - a legal opinion
laesa maiestas - law of treason
Lauricum - Lorch, Germany
legatus - legate
leges populi - laws made on behalf of the people
Levant - the eastern Mediterranean
Lex Julia - Julian law; in 18 BC, Augustus tried with this law to
  restore morality and encourage the birth of children
liberti - freedmen
libertas publica - public freedom
lictor - attendant of the magistrates
limes - the frontier
limites - limits of the frontier, boundaries
litterati - men of letters
Ludi Seculares - Secular Games
Lusitania - Portugal
Lyceum - a hall or school for learning
mare nostrum - our sea (the Mediterranean)
Mars Ultor - Mars the Avenger
mausoleum - large burial monument
Mausoleum Augusti - Mausoleum of Augustus
mens sana in corpore sano! - "a sound mind in a sound body"
Messiah - Redeemer
metae - end posts
Mi fili - "my child"
Moesia Inferior - lower Moesia, today Bulgaria
Moesia Superior - upper Moesia, today Serbia
monotheism - worship of one God
municipium - town
Napoli - Naples, Italy
nomenclator - someone who announces visitors or guests
Non fecit taliter omni nationi - "He did not do so much for every
  nation"
Noricum - part of Austria
numeri - units of 300 men from irregular forces and various
  ethnicities

Nymphaeum - Tivoli's moated pavilion with a large decorative
fountain
Omnia tendunt naturaliter in non esse - "All things tend
naturally toward disintegration"
Optimus - the best
palaestra - athletic field
panem et circenses - "bread and circuses"
Pannonia - Hungary
Pannonia Inferior - lower Pannonia, today it includes parts of
Hungary and Serbia
Pannonia Superior - upper Pannonia, today it includes parts of
Hungary, Serbia and Austria
Pantheon - the temple in Rome dedicated to all the gods of the
Empire
pantomimus - pantomime
papyrus - paper
Parthia capta - "Parthia captured"
pater - father
Pax Romana - Roman Peace
Penates - household gods
pedagogus puerorum - a teacher of the pages
perdidi diem! - "I have lost a day" (--Titus)
philhellenism - respect for Greek culture
pietas - dutifulness toward the family, the gods and the State;
piety
plebs - the general public
polytheism - belief in many gods
pomerium - boundary marker
Pons Aelius - a stately bridge at Newcastle, England
Pons Mulvius - the Mulvian Bridge (Rome)
Pontifex Maximus - high priest or chief priest
praefectus urbi - the prefect of Rome (Rome's police chief)
praefectus vehiculorum - transportation supervisor
praenomen - first name
praetor - judge
praetorianism - the interference by the military sector in the
government of a republic
prefecture - a district governed by a prefect
princeps - first citizen, i.e., the emperor
prudentes - jurists

quaestor - officer responsible for law and finance
qualis artifex pereo! - "what an artist perishes in me" (--Nero)
quid fecit senatus? - "What did the Senate do?"
Quod licet Iovi non licet bovi! - "What is permitted to Jupiter is not
    allowed to mere cattle."
Raetia - today parts of Germany and Austria
regina artium - rhetoric, the queen of arts
Res Gestae - Augustus's written accomplishments
respondit - "he answered"
responsa - legal opinion
Roma renascens - Rome reborn
Romanus sum - "I am a Roman"
rotunda - domed roof
saevitia - a jealous rage
Sarmizegetusa - Dacian capital in Romania
scolae - schools
senatus consultum - a special meeting or approval of the Senate
    (S.C.)
Senatus populusque Romanus - S.P.Q.R. - The Senate and the People
    of Rome
Serapeum - a semicircular building at Hadrian's villa
sestertius - sesterce; a quarter of a denarius, it was a coin of brass
    during the Empire
Sidon - Saida, Lebanon
signa - standards
silentiarius - one who kept the slaves silent
Singidunum - Belgrade, Serbia
spina - spine or center of the raceway
Superior et Inferior - the upper and lower, i.e., upriver and
    downriver
tablinum - office
Tellus - Mother Earth goddess
Templum Veneris et Romae - Hadrian's temple dedicated to Venus
    and Rome
tesserae - black and white mosaic patterned flooring
toga - a Roman male's ordinary clothing
toga virilis - toga of manhood
tomb of Domitii - now the Pincio Gardens (Rome)
trabae - a youth's white toga with purple stripe
tribunus - political officer

tribunus militum - military tribune
triclinium - dining room
Triumph - public celebration honoring a victorious general
Triumvirate - rule of three
tumulus - tomb
Turnu Severin - Drobeta, Romania
veni - "come here"
Vespasiani - contemporary term for restroom in Rome; named for
    Emperor Vespasian
vexillationes - small units from various legions
Via Sacra - Sacred Road (Rome)
Viminacium - Kostolac, Serbia
Vindobona - Vienna, Austria

Select Bibliography

Abbott, Frank Frost. The Common People of Ancient Rome: Studies of Roman Life and Literature. New York: Charles Scribner's Sons, 1911.

Africa, Thomas W. Rome of the Caesars. New York: Wiley, 1965.

The Ancients. Vol. IV. Chas. E. Merrill Publ. Co., 1968.

The Annals of Ancient Rome - Tacitus. Transl. by Michael Grant. New York: Barnes & Noble, Inc., 1963.

Bender, Henry V. The Civilization of Ancient Rome: An Archaeological Perspective - Beginnings to Augustus. Lanham, MD: University Press of America, Inc., 1985.

Benko, Stephen. Pagan Rome and the Early Christians. Bloomington, IN: Indiana University Press, 1984.

Birley, Anthony. Marcus Aurelius. Boston: Little, Brown and Company, 1966.

Boak, Arthur E.R. and William G. Sinnigen. A History of Rome to A.D. 565. 5th ed. New York: The Macmillan Co., 1965.

Bradley, K.R. Slaves and Masters in the Roman Empire: A Study in Social Control. New York: Oxford University Press, 1987.

Bury, J.B. A History of the Roman Empire: from its foundation to the death of Marcus Aurelius (27 B.C.-180 A.D.). New York: American Book Co. (n.d.)

Caesar, Julius. The Civil War. Trans. by Jane F. Mitchell. New York: Dorset Press, 1976.

Campbell, Brian. The Roman Army, 31 BC - AD 337: A Sourcebook. New York: Routledge, 1994.

Cary, M. A History of Rome: down to the reign of Constantine. London: Macmillan & Co., Ltd., 1962. 2nd ed. New York: St. Martin's Press, Inc.

Champlin, Edward. Fronto and Antonine Rome. Cambridge, MA: Harvard University Press, 1980.

Cook, S.A. et al. (eds.). The Imperial Peace, A.D. 70-192, in Cambridge Ancient History, XI. Cambridge, England: Cambridge University Press, 1936.

Cornell, Tim, and John Matthews. Atlas of the Roman World. New York: Facts on File, Inc., 1982.

Dill, Samuel. Roman Society: From Nero to Marcus Aurelius. Cleveland, OH: The World Publishing Co., 1956.

Durant, Will. Caesar and Christ. The Story of Civilization: Part III. New York: Simon and Schuster, 1944.

Empire Besieged - Time Frame A.D. 200-600. Alexandria, VA: Time- Life Books, 1988.

Farquharson, A.S.L. Marcus Aurelius: His Life and His World. Westport, CT: Greenwood Press, 1952.

Franzero, Carlo Maria. The Life and Times of Nero. New York: Philosophical Library, Inc., 1956.

Garnsey, Peter and Richard Saller. The Roman Empire: Economy, Society and Culture. Berkeley and Los Angeles, CA: University of California Press, 1987.

Garzetti, Albino. From Tiberius to the Antonines: A History of the Roman Empire, A.D. 14-192. Transl. by J. R. Foster. London: Methuen & Co., Ltd., 1960 and 1974.

Goodenough, Erwin R. The Church in the Roman Empire. New York: Henry Holt & Co., 1931.

Gordon, Arthur E. Illustrated Introduction to Latin Epigraphy. Berkeley, CA: University of California Press, 1983.

Grant, Michael. The Ancient Historians. New York: Charles Scribner & Sons, 1970.

Grant, Michael. Caesar. Chicago, IL: Follett Publ. Co., 1975.

Grant, Michael. The Founders of the Western World: A History of Greece and Rome. New York: Charles Scribner & Sons, 1991.

Grant, Michael. The Roman Emperors: a biographical guide to the rulers of imperial Rome. New York: Charles Scribner & Sons, 1985.

Grant, Michael. The Twelve Caesars. New York: Charles Scribner & Sons, 1975.

Grant, Michael. The Visible Past: Greek and Roman History from Archaeology 1960-1990. New York: Charles Scribner's Sons, 1990.

Grant, Michael. The World of Rome. Cleveland, OH: World Publ. Co., 1960.

Greenhalgh, P.A.L. The Year of the Four Emperors. London: Weidenfeld and Nicholson, 1975.

Hadas, Moses. Imperial Rome.
New York: Time-Life Books, 1965.

Heichelheim, Fritz M., Cedric A. Yeo and Allen M. Ward.
A History of the Roman People. 2nd ed. Englewood Cliffs,
NJ: Prentice-Hall, Inc., 1984.

Jones, A.H.M. (ed.). The Empire in A History of Rome Through the
Fifth Century, II. New York: Harper & Row, 1970.

Jones, Brian W. The Emperor Domitian.
New York: Routledge, 1992.

Jones, Brian W. The Emperor Titus.
New York: St. Martin's Press, 1984.

King, Anthony. Archaeology of Ancient Rome. New York: Crescent
Books, 1982.

Lambert, Royston. Beloved and God: The story of Hadrian and
Antinous. New York: Viking, 1984.

Levick, Barbara. Claudius. New Haven, CT: Yale University
Press, 1990.

Lewis, Naphtali and Meyer Reinhold (eds.). The Empire in Roman
Civilization, II. New York: Columbia University Press, 1955.

MacKendrick, Paul. The Mute Stones Speak: The Story of
Archaeology in Italy. New York: The New American Library,
1960.

McNeill, Wm. H. History of Western Civilization: A Handbook.
6th ed. Chicago, IL: University of Chicago Press, 1986.

Millar, Fergus. The Roman Empire and its Neighbors. Second ed.
New York: Holmes & Meier Publishers, Inc., 1981.

Miller, William. The Latins in the Levant. New York: Barnes &
Noble, Inc., 1964 reprint.

Muller, Herbert J. The Uses of the Past: Profiles of Former Societies. New York: Oxford University Press, 1952.

O'Grady, Desmond. The Victory of the Cross: A History of the Early Church in Rome. London: Harper Collins, 1992.

Perowne, Stewart. Hadrian. London: Croom Helm Ltd., 1960.

Petit, Paul. Pax Romana. Berkeley, CA: University of California Press, 1976.

Raaflaub, Kurt A. and Mark Toher (eds.). Between Republic and Empire: Interpretations of Augustus and His Principate. Berkeley: University of California Press, 1990.

Ramsey, W.M. The Church in the Roman Empire before A.D. 170. Grand Rapids, MI: Baker Book House, 1954.

Roberts, J.M. History of the World. New York: Knopf, 1976; Oxford University Press, 1993.

Rossi, Lino. Trajan's Column and the Dacian Wars. (English translation revised by J.M.C. Toynbee.) Ithaca, NY: Cornell University Press, 1971.

Sordi, Marta. The Christians and the Roman Empire. Transl. by Annabel Bedini. Norman, OK: University of Oklahoma Press, 1986.

Stark, Freya. Rome on the Euphrates. New York: Harcourt Brace & World, Inc., 1966.

Starr, Chester G. Civilization and the Caesars: The Intellectual Revolution in the Roman Empire. Ithaca, N.Y.: Cornell U. Press, 1954; Norton, 1965.

Starr, Chester G. A History of the Ancient World. 4th ed. New York: Oxford University Press, 1991.

Starr, Chester G. The Roman Empire, 27 B.C.-A.D. 476. New York: Oxford University Press, 1982.

Suetonius. The Twelve Caesars. Transl. by Robert Graves. New York: Penguin Books, 1957. Illustrated ed.

Syme, Sir Ronald. "Fictional History Old and New. Hadrian." James Bryce Memorial Lecture, 1984. Somerville College, 1986.

Syme, Sir Ronald. The Roman Revolution. Oxford University Press, 1960. Clarendon Press, 1939.

Tacitus, Cornelius. The Annals of Imperial Rome. Transl. by Michael Grant. New York: Penguin Books, 1976.

Vickers, Michael. The Roman World. New York: Peter Bedrick Books, 1989.

Von Hagen, Victor W. The Roads that Led to Rome. Cleveland, OH: World Publishing Co., 1967.

Watson, Paul Barron. Marcus Aurelius Antoninus. Freeport, NY: Books for Libraries Press (1971 Reprint) - first published in 1884.

Wheeler, Mortimer. Roman Art and Architecture. New York: Thames and Hudson, 1964.

INDEX

The triumph of Christianity is best viewed through buildings like the Baths of Diocletian. Last and largest of the baths, it became the Church of S. Maria dei Angeli y Martiris.

Hadrian (AD 117-38) was a larger-than-life emperor, reflected in the mausoleum he ordered built alongside the Tiber.

Fig. 1-2

The temple of Mars Ultor, vowed by Augustus in 42 BC at the battle of Philippi. Forum of Augustus.

Built to honor his divine ancestors, the temple sets on a raised platform reached by seventeen steps. Its fluted columns, surmounted by Corinthian Capitals, dwarf all other temple columns in Rome.

Fig. 3-4

The triumphal Arch of Constantine, AD 315.

M. Agrippa was both scientist, engineer, admiral and the son-in-law of Augustus. He built this temple just before his death at the age of fifty in 12 BC. It was rebuilt by Hadrian and became the Pantheon, one of the wonders of the Roman world.

Fig. 5-6

Lone sentinel to a distant past is all that remains of the once elegant Pons Aemilius. Dedicated in 142 BC, it was the first stone bridge to span the entire Tiber.

The mausoleum to Caesar Augustus was dedicated in 9 BC. It received his funerary urn in AD 14, as well as those of succeeding Julio-Claudian emperors and families.

Fig. 7-8

Marcus Aurelius (AD 161-80) adopted the virtues of Stoic philosophy as a youth. As emperor, he was forced to combat barbarian invasions. Gilded bronze equestrian statue. Capitoline Museum, Rome.

The Marcomannic Wars kept Marcus Aurelius camped along the Danube for more than ten years. In 174 the Senate and people of Rome raised the Column of Aurelius to honor the emperor known to history as the "last of the Good Emperors."

Fig. 9-10

The temple of Vesta harkens back to the primitive rounded huts of the eighth century BC's Romulus and Remus, twin survivors of Rome's first assassinations. Rebuilt several times, the last of which by Julia Domna, wife of Septimius Severus, in AD 204.--Forum Romanum.

Twin columns of the temple of the deified Vespasian, in the Forum. Begun by his son Titus (AD 79-81), it was completed by his brother Domitian (AD 81-96).

Fig. 11-12

Flames leapt high across this area of the city in AD 63, leading to Nero's ordering the ethnic cleansing of Christians. The next year he bought this land and had his domus aurea, "golden house," built, a lavish maze of halls and rooms with fountains cascading down marble walls into mosaic-lined pools.

Trajan (AD 98-117) was the consummate warrior-emperor. Born in Spain like his successor, Hadrian, he extended the boundaries of the Empire to their farthest limits. Trajan's Column depicts his Dacian wars (AD 102-06) in a scroll unfurling from the base of the column, sculpted with 12,000 figurines.

Fig. 13-14

The Colosseum was built by Vespasian and Titus, in the garden of Nero's domus aurea. In the foreground is the temple of Venus and Roma, largest in Rome, and probably designed by Hadrian.

The wooden flooring of the Colosseum was set at the level of the white marble to the left, then covered with sand.

Fig. 15-16

Hadrian was the supreme builder among all Roman emperors. His villa at Tivoli, outside Rome, reflected both his lengthy travels and eclectic spirit. View of pool and wall of poikele.

Alexandria, Egypt, was a brilliant metropolis that fell to the Romans with the death of Antony and Cleopatra. This enormous mosaic at Praeneste, Italy, depicts the city at the mouth of the Nile.

Fig. 17-18

The massive Aurelian Wall only delayed the eventual fall of the Imperial capital.

Looking east in the Forum to the triple arch of Septimius Severus, raised in AD 203 to commemorate the victories of his two sons over the Arabs and Parthians.

Fig. 19-20

The heart and soul of the Roman Empire was the Forum. The Senate House in the background was rebuilt in the third century AD and survived the centuries as an early Christian church.

The Fabrician Bridge, dedicated in 62 BC still functions today, connecting the left bank with Tiber Island.

Fig. 21-22

The town of Alba Fucens is nestled in Italy's mountains. With a little restoration the amphitheater could be functional again.

The vaulting of the Theater of Pompey hosts the restaurant San Pancrasio. The historic assassination on the Ides of March, 44 BC, took place in this stone theater.

Fig. 23-24

A river god bespeaks the idle decadence of Imperial Rome. Augustus strove to raise the morals of the capital, restoring 82 temples.

Rome's influence extended with its road-building. The Via Sacra, the holy road, winds through the Forum and up the Capitoline Hill to the temple of Jupiter, most renowned of Rome's temples.

Fig. 25-26

About the Author

The *Roman Empire* represents the first book on the subject for Mr. Schwartz. It was written, as was an earlier work, *Peru: Country in Search of a Nation* (1970), for both general reader and student.

The author is an ardent teacher and student of the past, particularly of civilizations that have left prominent cultural footprints that have maintained a continuous presence down to our time. In language, law, literature, art and architecture Rome has made of us its "virtual reality," in contemporary terms. The same is even more valid for the Inca Empire, whose descendants partake of ancestral values, of which he wrote in his first book on Peru.

Mr. Schwartz has lived, studied and explored in both of these bygone empires. His fascination with the past has taken him to all the major monuments of the regions, where he has developed respect for both people and cultures. He studied philosophy and languages at Sacred Heart Seminary in Ohio, sociology at St. Joseph College, Rensselaer and Whiting, Indiana, and Latin American Studies at Indiana University, Bloomington. His doctoral studies began at UCLA in Brazilian history, culminating at the University of Houston, where he took the Ph.D. in U.S. and Latin American history. Post-doctoral research was conducted at the American Academy in Rome (1990) through a Rockefeller Foundation fellowship for foreign language teachers. A Fulbright-Hays Seminars Abroad grant (1992) enabled him to study the language and culture of Brazil firsthand, from the forests of Amazonia to the dynamic cities of the south, and to write a brief history of Brazil for high school students (Fulbright Commission publication, 1993).

He spent the summer of 1997 researching the 17th century families of the Spanish conquistadors of Peru at the Archivo de Indias in Seville, Spain, through an independent study grant from the Council on Basic Education. In his search to awaken interest in the relationship between the values and traditions of the past and their importance to the present, Mr. Schwartz has explored the Spanish missions, from California to Florida. He has taught at all levels of learning in this country and Peru and continues to pursue the fascination of history as both teacher, scholar and traveler.